FAK

itsu

the cookbook

the cookbook

100 low-calorie eat beautiful recipes for health & happiness

Julian Metcalfe & Blanche Vaughan
Nutritional consultant Angela Dowden

MITCHELL BEAZLEY

itsu the cookbook
by Julian Metcalfe & Blanche Vaughan

First published in Great Britain in 2014 by Mitchell Beazley,
a division of Octopus Publishing Group Ltd, Endeavour House,
189 Shaftesbury Avenue, London WC2H 8JY
www.octopusbooks.co.uk

An Hachette UK Company
www.hachette.co.uk

ISBN: 978 1 84533 894 7

A CIP catalogue record for this book is available from the
British Library.

Set in VAG Rounded LT.

Printed and bound in China.

Publisher: Alison Starling
Art Director: Jonathan Christie
Deputy Art Director: Yasia Williams-Leedham
Senior Editor: Leanne Bryan
Designer: Jaz Bahra
Illustrator: Abigail Read
Assistant Production Manager: Caroline Alberti

Copy Editor: Trish Burgess
Proofreader: Jane Bamforth
Indexer: Isobel McLean
Photographer: Anders Schønnemann
Food Stylist: Annie Rigg
Assistant Food Stylist: Miranda Keyes
Nutritional Consultant: Angela Dowden
Props Stylists: Tabitha Hawkins and Jessica Georgiades

Notes:

Unless stated otherwise in the recipes:

- All calorie counts and fat content figures are per serving.
- All spoon measures are level.
- All eggs are medium.
- All vegetables should be peeled, as necessary.
- All herbs and leaves should be washed and trimmed, as necessary.
- Chillis can be used with or without seeds, depending on how spicy you like your food.
- Standard bunches of herbs are 20g, small bunches are 10g, and large bunches are 30g.

This book contains some dishes made with raw or lightly cooked eggs. It is prudent for more vulnerable people, such as pregnant and nursing mothers, people with weakened immune systems, the elderly, babies and young children, to avoid dishes made with uncooked or lightly cooked eggs.

Contents

Introduction

Like itsu, this book has been years in the making. We hope you find it inspirational and practical in equal measure!

The early pioneers of Pret A Manger are the creative force behind itsu. We opened our first award-winning restaurant on Brompton Cross, Chelsea, London in 1997. Years of listening and reacting to customers encouraged us to battle on and build a new type of food place dedicated to skinny but delicious food.

Over time, with untold hard work and passion, we morphed into an extremely busy, lighteningly fast take-out place with thousands of discerning, loyal customers. We have managed to open a further 50 itsu shops so far, many with lots of seats.

We still run our conveyor-belt restaurants with pride; we now call them itsu [dining] to distinguish them from our shops.

We have, almost by accident, become the world's first EAT BEAUTIFUL healthy fast-food bar… light, green and good for you. Apparently the secret to Pink Floyd's breathtaking music is as much about what they left out as what they put in, a bit like itsu: less fat, more bounce.

itsu pays homage to the remarkable cuisine of Japan, Korea, Vietnam and Thailand – restaurant food, street food, chefs' food, home-cooked food – and many of the recipes that we serve in our shops and restaurants appear in this, our first cookbook. The recipes are light – all under 300 calories per person – and packed full of essential nutritional goodness.

Thank you to all our customers, inspiring management and amazing staff for making itsu possible.

Endless gratitude to Blanche Vaughan, Celeste Tobias-Metcalfe, Pippi Brereton, William Da Silva, Tania Betley and Nicola Formby for making this book a reality.

Julian Metcalfe

Founder of itsu, co-founder of Pret A Manger

itsu orchids are fresh & beautiful
(a bit like our food...)

White orchids, in particular,
signify luxury & love.

The word orchid comes from
the Greek 'orkhis' meaning testicle...
on account of the shape of
its tuberous roots.

How to eat the itsu way

If you care about your body, you'll care about what you eat. At itsu we know that fabulous-tasting food can be good for you, too, and the totally delicious recipes in this book prove our point.

Our formula is really simple: healthy + delicious = itsu. We take unprocessed raw ingredients that are naturally high in flavour while being low in saturated fat and calories (rather than artificially manipulated to be so), cook them simply and quickly, and serve them fresh.

The good news is that, even if you don't eat or cook the itsu way every day, you can still adopt the underlying principles and make significant changes to your health while keeping your tastebuds happy too. Here's how to incorporate some healthy eating into your life…

Embrace the Asian influence

The Japanese diet contains lots of heart-healthy oily fish, plenty of high-protein, isoflavone-rich soya foods (some researchers believe that isoflavones help balance female hormones) and a smattering of iodine-packed seaweeds that can promote a healthy metabolic rate. So whether it's swapping a burger for a salmon steak, helping yourself to a bit of nori-wrapped sushi for lunch, or popping some edamame beans into your salad, there are many ways you can and should incorporate an Asian theme in your diet.

A touch of *hara hachi bu*, which means 'belly 80 per cent full', is another Japanese habit that's well worth adopting. The idea is to stop eating before you're fit to burst, which can only be a good thing for your waistline and overall well-being.

Eat good fat

Having a healthy fat intake doesn't mean depriving yourself of every high-fat food, but it does mean moderating how much you consume and choosing the healthier types when you do indulge. This means that, while you might choose to eat less butter, cream and red meat, you can enjoy healthy quantities of lovely nuts and seeds, oil-based dressings, avocados and oily fish. By doing so, you'll be reducing your intake of saturated fat, which can contribute to clogged arteries, while ensuring you get enough of the fats that are actively good for your heart. Plant and marine oils also provide the essential fatty acids that help nerve cells to communicate with each other and keep your skin healthy, thereby beautifying you from the inside out.

Moderate those carbs

When it comes to carbohydrates, it's good not to make them the focus of every meal (although current UK government advice says otherwise, which many consider outdated). But it's also good not to be completely carb-phobic (in an equally old-hat Atkins-esque sort of way). Instead, and in keeping with the itsu philosophy of food, the focus should be on having no more than fist-sized portions of nutritious carbs, such as noodles, beans, pitta bread, wholewheat pasta and brown rice. By doing this, and by avoiding too many high glycaemic index (GI) foods, such as sugars and refined starches, which give you a quick energy boost followed by an equally rapid slump,

itsu puddings   2.50

vitsu water   1.65
under 60 calories!

you'll avoid constantly flash-flooding your system with high levels of glucose and insulin. The happy result? You will decrease your risk of diabetes and heart disease, and find it easier to manage your weight.

Choose satisfying food

Managing your weight is all about feeling fuller on fewer calories and triggering the body's satiety signals, which is exactly what the recipes in this book achieve. Half the secret lies in eating mountains of crunchy and delicious vegetables, salads and pulses that score low on the energy-density scale (a fancy way of saying that they provide lots of stomach-filling bulk but few calories). The other half of the secret is in having a good helping of lean protein, such as chicken, prawns, eggs or edamame beans, which we all tend to agree transform a less-than-filling snack into a proper meal. There's a good reason for this, as protein has been scientifically proved to be the most satisfying nutrient. It's the perfect excuse for tucking into some of your favourite foods.

Eat a rainbow

Brightly coloured fruit and vegetables are particularly important sources of the antioxidants that can mop up cell-damaging free radicals. And those lovely shades of orange, red and purple are so gorgeously vibrant – one of the reasons many itsu dishes look so beautiful – that they'll cheer you up by just looking at them. In short, don't stop at just eating your greens: try to eat a rainbow of goodness too.

Sprinkle some seedy goodness

You'll notice that many itsu recipes include a little sprinkle of super-healthy seeds. That's because they not only add some crunch but, from a nutritional perspective, they punch well

above their very meagre weight. As a rule, seeds are good at making up the shortfall of valuable minerals that can sometimes be difficult to obtain in sufficient amounts from other sources. From the itsu storecupboard, just 1 tablespoon of sesame seeds provides around one-tenth of the recommended daily allowance (RDA) of magnesium, while 1 tablespoon of pumpkin seeds supplies a similar amount of the zinc RDA. Other great salad and soup sprinkles that can effortlessly increase your nutritional intake include finely chopped Brazil nuts (rich in selenium and magnesium), pine nuts (high in zinc) and hemp seeds (loaded with magnesium and iron).

And a little bit of what you fancy…

Last but not least, the itsu philosophy allows for some decadent treats. A little bit of what you fancy can only do you good. Using better ingredients with more intense flavours is the key to doing this well. For example, good-quality chocolate (containing 70 per cent cocoa solids, as opposed to about 20 per cent in ordinary milk chocolate) offers a more satisfying hit, so you can eat less while losing none of the enjoyment. Savour every mouthful, and remember that small can be beautiful.

Our recipes

If you've enjoyed eating at itsu when you're out and about, this book now gives you 100 ways to recreate that dining experience in your own home. All the recipes within these pages – many of them itsu classics – are under 300 calories per serving, and the vast majority are low in saturated fat. Whether you're looking to feel more energetic, lose a few pounds (the recipes will fit neatly into a 5:2-style fasting regime), or just feel a bit brighter and lighter, eating well has never been easier or tastier.

Glossary of terms & ingredients

Bonito flakes (*katsuobushi*) – these are shavings made from dried, smoked fillets of bonito fish, which looks like tuna but is actually related to mackerel. Bonito flakes can be bought in airtight containers and are used for making *dashi*, or to sprinkle over food as a flavoursome seasoning.

Dashi – a Japanese stock made from *kombu* and *bonito flakes* that are steeped in boiled water. Dashi plays a very important part in Japanese cooking and is used in a wide variety of dishes, including soups, sauces, dips and omelette mixtures. You can make your own (*see* page 165), or buy instant dashi in sachets from Japanese food shops or online.

Edamame – small green soya beans bought in or out of the pod. They are available fresh or frozen from large supermarkets. High in protein, these beans can also help to regulate cholesterol levels.

Furikake – a Japanese seasoning made from black and white sesame seeds, ground *nori* and dried red *shiso* leaves. Delicious sprinkled over everything from rice to cooked fish or salads.

Ginger – fresh or pickled, this warming spice has traditionally been used to boost circulation, ease joints and aid digestion. In Japan people like to eat pickled ginger between mouthfuls of sushi to cleanse the palate. Pickled ginger is readily available in most supermarkets – good brands to look out for are Clearspring and Yutaka.

Glass noodles – made from rice, these dried noodles have a translucent quality, hence their name. They come in various thicknesses, and our recipes use fine ones (resembling angel hair pasta) or flat ones (resembling tagliatelle).

Glycaemic Index (GI) – a measure of how quickly a carbohydrate-containing food raises blood sugar levels. High GI carbs are rapidly broken down and assimilated, giving a big spike in sugar levels that may be followed by a slump; lower GI carbs are generally thought of as healthier because they give steadier sugar and energy levels and may fill you up for longer.

Japanese rice – *see* Sushi rice.

Kombu – a dried dark green seaweed that may be reconstituted in water. It is a good source of minerals, especially iodine, and adds *umami* flavouring to soups and stocks.

Maki – rolled sushi (*see* pages 54–61).

Matcha – a powder made from ground green tea leaves; it is used in tea ceremonies or as a flavouring to make *mochi* (pounded sticky rice sweets) and green tea ice cream.

Mirin – low-alcohol sweet rice wine (usually 8–10 per cent proof) used only for cooking. It is pale, with a slightly syrupy texture.

Miso – a paste made from fermented soya beans, this is used for everything from soups and dressings to marinades, dips and even puddings. There are many types of miso: white (*shiro miso*) is the most commonly used and has a soft, sweet flavour; red or dark (*aka miso*) is richer and saltier; miso made from brown rice (*genmai miso*) is a recent development, and well worth trying.

Noodles – *see* Glass noodles, Soba noodles and Udon noodles.

Nori – dried seaweed sheets used for wrapping sushi such as maki (*see* pages 54–61). It is highly nutritious, rich in protein, vitamins and minerals, including iodine. Nori is also delicious torn up or crumbled and sprinkled over food as a seasoning. Alternatively, blitz a sheet in a food processor or blender and add the flakes to toasted sesame seeds to make your own *furikake*.

Oil – the most commonly used oil for cooking in Japan is rice bran oil, but this is hard to find in the UK, so groundnut, sunflower or rapeseed oils can be used instead. Light olive oil or a vegetable oil are often used for dressings, but sesame oil, rapeseed, grapeseed and hemp oil may be used too. Using a variety of oils in your diet means that you will get a good balance of healthy fats and antioxidants, such as vitamin E.

Potsu – the generic word for a sauce or sauced dish.

Rice – *see* Sushi rice.

Rice vinegar – made from brown or white rice, rice vinegar is essential for seasoning sushi rice and is used in many dressings and sauces. It has excellent anti-bacterial properties, and is also used to preserve cooked sushi rice. Rice vinegar can reduce the GI of the rice you eat, and thereby help to keep energy levels more consistent. When consumed in a pickle at the end of a meal, it reputedly has digestive benefits.

Sake – Japanese rice wine (16–20 per cent proof), which can be drunk hot or cold, and is the perfect drink to accompany sushi. An inexpensive sake is fine for cooking purposes, and a dry sherry can be used instead. Sake has fewer calories than gin or vodka.

Sashimi – extremely fresh fish or meat sliced very thinly into bite-sized pieces.

Seaweed – *see* Kombu and Nori.

Sesame oil – there are two types – toasted and untoasted. The untoasted oil has a delicate flavour; it can be used for frying but has a low burning point, so care should be taken. The toasted oil is stronger and is best used as a condiment or for dressings so that its distinctive, nutty flavour isn't destroyed. It can also be poured over dishes to finish them.

Sesame seeds – black sesame seeds, or toasted white sesame seeds, are great for sprinkling over salads, meat or fish to give them extra texture and crunch. The toasted variety may be hard to find in UK supermarkets, but it's very easy to toast the seeds yourself in a dry frying pan, and

doing so does make a real flavour difference. As well as tasting nutty and delicious, sesame seeds help to lower cholesterol and strengthen the blood vessels, and are a great source of calcium, magnesium, iron and zinc.

Shichimi – also known as 'seven-flavour chilli pepper', this is a hot, spiced powder used for sprinkling over dishes to add some fragrant heat. It usually contains a mixture of ground chilli, ground sanshō, citrus zest, sesame seeds, hemp seeds, ginger and *nori*. As an alternative, you could use hot chilli flakes instead.

Shiitake mushrooms – fresh shiitake have a deep, meaty flavour and are readily available in large supermarkets. Dried shiitake can be used instead; just reconstitute them in boiling water for 20 minutes.

Shiso – a green or red herb, sometimes called 'perilla', which is a member of the mint family. It has many uses, and is a constituent of *furikake* seasoning.

Soba noodles – often made from a mixture of wheat and buckwheat flour, these noodles can also be 100 per cent buckwheat, which makes them gluten-free. Bought dried, they are thin, like spaghetti, and are cooked in just the same way – for a few minutes in boiling water. They can be eaten hot with broth, or cold as a salad. Noodles, both *udon* and soba, but especially the buckwheat ones, are low GI, which means they release energy slowly and steadily – much better than quick sugar highs.

Soya beans – *see* Edamame.

Soy sauce – one of the most important ingredients in Japanese cooking, this sauce is made from fermented soya beans and replaces salt in many recipes. Dark soy, which is used more often than light soy, is slightly richer and sweeter, but less salty.

Sugar alternatives – agave, coconut sugar, fruit sugar, stevia and xylitol are all good alternatives to white caster or granulated sugar. Brown sugar alternatives include brown rice syrup, date sugar, honey, maple syrup or palm sugar.

Sushi-grade fish – this simply means very fresh seafood from safe, reliable sources. Sushi-grade tuna, for example, has often been blast-frozen for 30 minutes at source to destroy any potential bacteria or parasites. It's always advisable to use a good fishmonger if you want to find really fresh fish for making sushi. Supermarkets now stock excellent-quality fish, but may not be able to offer 'sushi-grade' because the term is a general description rather than a precise definition. At itsu we care about sustainability, and all our tuna is supported by the Sustainable Fisheries Partnership's FishSource database (www.fishsource.com).

Sushi rice – short-grain rice, also known as Japanese rice, used for sushi. When cooked, this is stickier and softer than long-grain rice, and can be formed into shapes that hold together well. Brown sushi rice is a good alternative to the usual white polished variety because it contains more valuable nutrients. Rice is gluten-free, contains energizing complex carbohydrates and virtually no fat.

Tahini – a paste made from ground sesame seeds. Asian sesame paste is often made using unhulled seeds, so it has a darker colour and rougher texture than that used in Greek, Turkish and Middle Eastern cooking. The latter type, which is lighter and smoother, is easier to find in UK supermarkets. Either variety can be used in our recipes.

Tamari – a wheat-free alternative to *soy sauce*. High in protein, magnesium, potassium and iron, it can be used instead of soy in all the recipes if you are gluten intolerant.

Tobiko – red/orange flying fish roe. It has a mildly salty taste and crunchy texture, and is used on the outside of some sushi rolls. It is also excellent as one of the ingredients inside a hand roll (*see* page 64). A good alternative is salmon roe, though the eggs are slightly larger.

Tofu – also known as bean curd, tofu is made from cooked soya beans pressed into blocks. It can be soft/silken with a texture like custard (good for dressings and sauces) or firm/cotton (good for slicing). It is a great alternative to meat, eggs or dairy produce and is suitable for vegetarians, vegans and those who are lactose intolerant.

Udon noodles – thick wheat noodles, often served in a broth. You can buy them dried or ready-cooked (instant).

Umami – the fifth taste sensation in addition to sweet, sour, bitter and salty. Umami describes the deeply savoury or 'meaty' flavours found in foods containing glutamate, a naturally occurring amino acid. These foods include mushrooms, ripe tomatoes, soy sauce and preserved fish – anchovies and dried bonito flakes, for example – as well as cured meats and Parmesan cheese.

Wakame – means sesame seaweed, which gives you an idea of the flavour. It can be bought dried and shredded, and reconstituted in cold water in just 5 minutes. Often used in salads and many miso-based soups, it is very rich in iodine, which is important for a healthy thyroid gland.

Wasabi – a horseradish-like plant that is native to Japan and grows in fresh mountain streams. It is hard to find fresh wasabi in the UK (and it can be very expensive), but you can use the cheaper and more readily available powdered form (add water and make a paste) or buy it ready-mixed in tubes. Both are very hot, so must be added carefully. Fresh horseradish can be used as an alternative.

Yuzu – a fruit that looks like a small, knobbly grapefruit and tastes tart but sweet, similar to a mandarin. It is difficult to find fresh yuzu in the UK, but bottles of Yutaka brand yuzu juice can be bought online or from good Japanese food shops. Alternatively, use mandarin juice mixed with a little lemon and lime juice. Yuzu is a wonderfully antioxidant citrus fruit, containing three times more vitamin C than a lemon.

USEFUL EQUIPMENT

Bamboo steamer – for cooking vegetables, because steaming preserves more of the nutrients than boiling.

Blender – a jug blender or stick blender work for all the recipes in this book.

Garlic press – for crushing garlic if you'd rather do this than grate it.

Grater – with large holes for grating ginger and small holes for grating garlic.

Heavy-based saucepan with lid – essential for perfect Japanese-style rice.

Measuring spoons – regular cutlery varies in size but the exact quantity for a tablespoon is 15ml and a teaspoon is 5ml. Use these when measuring for best results.

Sharp knives – essential for cutting fish, and for making all sorts of chopping easier and quicker.

Sushi mat – made of thin bamboo sticks and essential for making maki rolls.

Timer – for cooking rice with perfect precision.

Storecupboard essentials

Here are some useful ingredients to keep in stock so that you can make the recipes in this book whenever you like. They all have a long shelf-life and most of them are easy to find in large supermarkets. Alternatively, buy them online (*see* page 188) or from good Japanese food shops.

1   **Rice vinegar** – Yutaka, Clearspring and Waitrose are all good brands.

2   **Miso paste** – Clearspring make a good white miso paste. *See* page 12 for varieties available in the supermarket.

3   **Fish sauce** – we recommend Squid brand or Waitrose's own.

4   **Kombu** – Large thick strips of dried seaweed. Used to make dashi stock as well as a seasoning for dressings and sauces. Available online or from Japanese food shops.

5   **Wasabi** – powdered; look for Clearspring or S&B, available from specialist Japanese food shops and websites.

6   **Wakame** – this dried seaweed may be hard to find in supermarkets, so look online or in Japanese food shops for the Wel Pac brand.

7   **Tofu** – it's useful to have both soft and firm varieties in your storecupboard.

8   **Bonito flakes** – flakes of smoked, dried fish used to season stocks and sauces. Available in airtight bags, which store well. Buy them online or from Japanese food shops.

9   **Sushi rice** – a short-grain rice. Look for a 'premium quality' brand labelled as sushi rice.

10 **Pickled ginger** – Clearspring and Yutaka are both good brands.

11 **Mirin** – sweet rice wine vinegar; Waitrose's own brand is good.

12 **Soy sauce** – we recommend the Kikkoman brand of both soy and gluten-free soy (tamari).

13 **Toasted sesame seeds** – if you can't find these, it's easy to toast ordinary sesame seeds in a hot, dry frying pan.

14 **Nori** – dried seaweed sheets made by Clearspring are available in large supermarkets.

15 **Crystal roll wrappers** – rice paper for spring rolls (also known as spring roll or rice wrappers) available from Waitrose, Asian supermarkets or online.

Chicken stock – for instant chicken stock we recommend Knorr Stock Pot.

Dashi powder – instant dashi, also called *hon dashi* or *dashi no moto*, is available online or from specialist Japanese suppliers.

Groundnut oil – or other light cooking oil, such as grapeseed, sunflower or vegetable oil.

Noodles – keep a stock of glass noodles in two thicknesses (very fine, resembling angel hair, and wider, resembling tagliatelle), plus udon and soba noodles. Clearspring is a good brand for these last two types.

Sake – choose an inexpensive variety, or use dry sherry as an alternative.

Sesame oil – try to find pure sesame oil rather than toasted; it has a delicately nutty flavour and is delicious in dressings.

Sugar alternatives – agave, coconut sugar, palm sugar, stevia and xylitol are all good alternatives to granulated and caster sugar.

USEFUL FRESH INGREDIENTS

Fresh root ginger, garlic, hot red Thai chillies, lemons, limes and spring onions.

SOUPS }

» • 93 calories
• 0.7g saturated fat

Simple miso soup

In Japan people love miso soup so much that they even eat it for breakfast. We're not stopping you! At itsu you can even buy sachets of ready-mixed miso paste – just add hot water and tofu for a very quick version of this soup. Instant dashi (just add boiling water) is also available in neat little sachets, so it's easy to keep some in the cupboard (*see* page 188 for stockists).

Serves 4 as a small bowl

800ml instant dashi, Homemade Dashi Stock (*see* page 165) or water

3 tbsp white miso paste

100g firm tofu, cut into cubes

large pinch of dried wakame, soaked in cold water for 5 minutes, then drained

2 spring onions, sliced

1   Bring the stock to a simmer. Put the miso in a cup or small bowl and mix in a tablespoon of the hot stock to soften it slightly and make a smooth liquid paste. Stir the paste into the stock until dissolved.

2   Put the tofu and wakame in the bottom of 4 serving bowls and pour over the hot soup. Sprinkle with the spring onions to serve.

{ **Nutritional tip:** Miso is a paste made from fermented soya beans, and is rich in probiotic bacteria, which means it's good for intestinal health.

Variation: Try foamed soya milk as a topping for a miso cappuccino.

» • 269 calories
• 3.9g saturated fat

Smoked mackerel miso soup

Add a smoky note to a simple miso soup – and some extra health benefits too.

Serves 4 as a starter or 2 as a main course

800ml instant dashi, Homemade Dashi Stock (*see* page 165) or water

3 tbsp white miso paste

100g smoked mackerel, skinned and flaked into small pieces

100g firm tofu, cut into cubes

large pinch of dried wakame, soaked in cold water for 5 minutes, then drained

1 spring onion, sliced

1   Bring the stock to a simmer. Put the miso in a cup or small bowl and mix in a tablespoon of the hot stock to soften it slightly and make a smooth liquid paste. Stir the paste into the stock until dissolved.

2   Equally divide the mackerel, tofu and wakame between serving bowls and pour over the hot miso stock. Sprinkle with the spring onion and serve piping hot.

{ **Nutritional tip:** Mackerel is one of the finest sources of omega-3 oils, which fight inflammation and help to keep the heart and brain healthy.

Variation: Turn the soup into more of a meal by adding sliced shiitake mushrooms, leeks or baby spinach leaves.

Simple miso soup

- 45 calories
- 3g saturated fat

Dynamite broth
We never use dashi that contains monosodium glutamate (MSG) when we make this soup at itsu. We think this flavour-enhancing chemical is quite unnecessary, so if you buy dashi rather than make it, do look out for one that's MSG-free. We use dashi as the basis of potsu (sauce) recipes, as well as in our Detox Soup (*see* page 24). The broth will keep for up to a week in the fridge, and also freezes well, so you can always have some on hand to make a quick soup.

Serves 4

1.6 litres instant dashi, Homemade Dashi Stock (*see* page 165) or water

5 tbsp white miso paste

2 tbsp coconut milk

1 tbsp mirin

20g or 4cm fresh root ginger, grated

1 tsp tamarind paste

1 garlic clove, grated or crushed

4 lime leaves, chopped

1 hot red Thai chilli, finely chopped

1   Bring the stock to a simmer. Put the miso in a cup or small bowl and mix in a tablespoon of the hot stock to soften it slightly and make a smooth liquid paste. Stir the paste into the stock until dissolved.

2   Put all the remaining ingredients into a blender and blitz to combine. Pour into the hot stock and simmer for about 5 minutes to allow the flavours to develop. (If you don't have a blender, just chop the vegetables into smaller pieces at the beginning and omit this step.)

3   Use immediately or cool and store in the fridge for up to a week.

- 200 calories
- 1.7g saturated fat

Detox soup

A favourite itsu lunchtime soup, this is full of delicious vegetables and filling noodles. You'll get two antioxidant-packed vegetable portions, and a good amount of satisfying protein from each bowl. It's hard to find a healthier way to fill up! If you like, you can use a handful of each vegetable instead of weighing it.

Serves 4

1 quantity Dynamite Broth (*see* page 23)

1 red pepper, cored and deseeded

100g or a handful of green beans, topped

100g or a handful of carrots

100g or a handful of mangetout

100g or a handful of shiitake mushrooms

100g or a handful of spinach

100g or a handful of bean sprouts

200g firm tofu, cut into cubes

3 tbsp wakame, soaked in cold water
for 5 minutes, then drained

40g thin glass noodles, soaked in boiling
water for 5 minutes, then drained

Nutritional tip: Wakame is a type of seaweed, very rich in iodine, which is important for a healthy thyroid gland; the tofu in this soup also adds lean protein, good for filling you up without piling on the pounds.

1   Bring the broth to a simmer. Meanwhile, cut all the vegetables, apart from the spinach and bean sprouts, into bite-sized pieces.

2   Add all the chopped vegetables and boil for 2½ minutes, then add the spinach and bean sprouts for 30 seconds.

3   Put the tofu, wakame and noodles in the bottom of each bowl and ladle over the vegetables and hot broth.

- 300 calories
- 2.7g saturated fat

Easy chicken pho
This noodle dish, eaten all across Vietnam, is growing so popular in the UK that there's even a restaurant chain named after it. The recipe is a refreshingly skinny blend of fragrant spices and herbs in a healthy ginger-infused broth. With juicy chicken pieces, naturally gluten-free glass noodles and crisp bean sprouts, this is a dish that's true to our aim and butterfly light.

Serves 2

1 white onion, halved

20g or 4cm fresh root ginger, thickly sliced

800ml chicken stock

1 tsp coriander seeds

4 cloves

2 star anise

½ cinnamon stick

small bunch of coriander

2 boneless, skinless chicken thighs

2 tsp palm sugar or brown sugar alternative

1 tbsp fish sauce

salt

TO SERVE

50g flat rice noodles, soaked in boiling water for 15 minutes (or according to packet instructions)

2 large handfuls of bean sprouts

1 red onion, finely sliced

big handful of mixed coriander (reserved from small bunch above), basil and mint leaves, roughly chopped

1 hot red Thai chilli, finely chopped

juice of ½ lime

1 Heat a dry, heavy-based frying pan until very hot. Char the onion and ginger in it for 4 minutes each side. This adds a wonderful depth of flavour, but if you're in a hurry, you can skip this step.

2 Put the stock in a saucepan with the onion, ginger, spices and coriander stems (reserve the leaves) and bring to the boil. Add the chicken thighs and cook for 15 minutes. Lift the chicken out with a slotted spoon and allow to cool slightly before slicing into bite-sized pieces.

3 Strain the stock into a bowl, discarding the solids, then return to the pan. Add salt to taste, then the sugar, fish sauce and chicken pieces.

4 To serve, put the rice noodles into bowls and ladle over the hot stock and chicken. Sprinkle over the bean sprouts, red onion, herbs, chilli and lime juice, or offer these separately for the diners to add themselves.

Nutritional tip: Fresh coriander contains as much vitamin C as citrus fruit.

- 189 calories
- 8.2g saturated fat

Squash, spinach & coconut soup with ginger

Full of goodness and warmth, this soup is quick and easy to make, and can be a great vegetarian option too – just use vegetable stock rather than chicken. The creamy coconut, soothing ginger and crunch of bamboo shoots make it very satisfying.

Serves 4

1 litre chicken stock

200ml coconut milk

1 hot red Thai chilli, finely chopped

20g or 4cm fresh root ginger, finely chopped

1 tbsp soy sauce

1 tbsp fish sauce

2 tsp lemon juice

1 tsp cornflour

500g butternut squash, deseeded and cut into 1cm cubes

about 250g spinach leaves

about 150g bamboo shoots, rinsed, or 150g baby corn, chopped

1 Bring the stock to the boil in a large saucepan and add the coconut milk, chilli, ginger, soy sauce and fish sauce.

2 Mix the lemon juice with the cornflour in a cup or bowl to form a smooth paste. Stir the paste into the stock and cook at a gentle boil for 5 minutes.

3 Add the squash to the stock and continue to boil gently for 5–7 minutes, until tender.

4 Stir in the spinach and cook for another minute, or until just wilted.

5 Blend briefly to make a deliciously creamy soup with a slightly chunky texture. (If you don't have a blender, just chop the vegetables into smaller pieces at the beginning and omit this step.)

6 Finally, stir in the bamboo shoots or baby corn and heat through to serve.

- 117 calories
- 1.9g saturated fat

Egg drop soup with shiitake mushrooms Incredibly easy
to put together, this is a favourite storecupboard supper among young
Japanese – and it's great on a budget too. It provides all the nutrients
you need and is full of flavour and wonderfully satisfying.

Serves 2

500ml instant dashi, Homemade Dashi Stock
(see page 165) or water

100g shiitake mushrooms, finely chopped ....

2 eggs

1 tbsp soy sauce, plus extra to serve (optional)

1 tbsp mirin

sprigs of coriander, to garnish (optional)

Variations: Dried shiitake can be used
instead of fresh, but remember to soak
them first for 20 minutes in boiling water.
Alternatively, use edamame (soya) beans,
or other small vegetables, such as peas
or chopped asparagus.

1   Bring the stock to the boil. Add the mushrooms and cook for 3 minutes.

2   Whisk the eggs with the soy sauce and mirin, then stir into the stock. They will form
beautiful strands in the hot liquid.

3   Serve piping hot garnished with coriander sprigs, if liked, with extra soy sauce as
seasoning, if required.

- 194 calories
- 1.4g saturated fat

Hot & sour soup with pork & noodles

Low in calories but really filling, this is a great soup to take into the office and reheat for lunch. Any leftovers are great for a quick, ready-made supper.

Serves 4

100g mixed mushrooms (shiitake, oyster or enoki work well)

100g thin glass noodles, soaked in boiling water for 5 minutes, then drained

100g minced pork

2 spring onions, sliced

small handful of coriander, chopped

lime wedges (optional)

BROTH

1.5 litres chicken stock

½ tsp salt

1 hot red Thai chilli, sliced in half lengthways

1 tsp palm sugar or brown sugar alternative

juice of 1 lime

1 lemon grass stalk, finely chopped

4 lime leaves

2 tbsp fish sauce

1 First make the broth. Bring the stock to the boil, then add all the other broth ingredients and simmer for a few minutes to infuse.

2 Add the mushrooms, noodles and pork, stirring well to break up the meat, and cook for 3–4 minutes.

3 Serve with the spring onions and coriander sprinkled on top and, if you wish, a wedge of lime on the side.

Variation: Try making this with prawns instead of pork – a delicious (and still skinny) alternative.

- 182 calories
- 1g saturated fat

Hot & sour prawn soup
The delicious fragrant flavours of lemon grass, lime and hot chilli make this a fully balanced yet pure-tasting soup.

Serves 2

800ml chicken stock

½ tsp salt

½–1 hot red Thai chilli (depending on preference)

1 tsp palm sugar or brown sugar alternative

3 tbsp lime juice

1 lemon grass stalk, finely chopped

4 lime leaves

2 tbsp fish sauce

100g shiitake mushrooms, sliced

150g uncooked peeled prawns

TO SERVE

2 spring onions, finely chopped

sprigs of coriander

lime wedges

1 Bring the stock to the boil. Add all the other ingredients except the prawns, and simmer for 5 minutes.

2 Add the prawns and cook for 2 minutes, until they turn pink.

3 Ladle the soup into bowls and serve with the spring onions and coriander on top, plus a lime wedge alongside for extra zing.

- 222 calories
- 2.3g saturated fat

Hot & sour lemon grass chicken soup

Here's a fragrant soup that is hot, sour, salty and sweet all at once. It's filling, healthy and easy to make. itsu chefs prefer chicken thigh meat in soups and potsus because it's juicer than breast and gives a better flavour.

Serves 4

1.5 litres chicken stock

1 tsp palm sugar or brown sugar alternative

20g or 4cm fresh root ginger, sliced

1 lemon grass stalk, chopped

2 shallots, sliced

4 lime leaves

1 tsp tamarind paste

2 boneless, skinless chicken thighs

juice of 1 lime

2 tbsp fish sauce

1 hot red Thai chilli, deseeded and roughly chopped (optional)

small bunch of coriander, roughly chopped

1   Put the stock into a saucepan with the sugar, ginger, lemon grass, shallots, lime leaves and tamarind paste. Bring to the boil, then add the chicken and simmer for 15 minutes.

2   Using a slotted spoon, remove the chicken from the stock and set aside to cool slightly. Strain the stock, discarding the solids, then return it to the saucepan.

3   When cool enough to handle, shred or slice the chicken into bite-sized pieces and add to the stock with the lime juice, fish sauce, chilli (if using) and coriander. Ladle into bowls to serve.

- 224 calories
- 9.7g saturated fat

Chicken, mushroom & coconut soup
This velvety blend of chicken and creamy coconut is deeply satisfying but skinny too, and any leftovers will keep well in the fridge.

Serves 4

1 litre chicken stock

200ml coconut milk

1 hot red Thai chilli, deseeded and finely chopped

200g mixed mushrooms (shiitake, oyster, enoki or buna shimeji work well)

4 lime leaves

150g boneless, skinless chicken thighs

150g mixture of pak choi, sugarsnap peas, spinach and baby corn, or a small handful of each

1 tbsp fish sauce

1 tsp palm sugar or brown sugar alternative

1 tbsp lime juice

small bunch of coriander, roughly chopped, to serve

Nutritional tip: Coconut is a great source of iron, potassium and zinc. Like seeds and avocado, coconut milk is naturally high in saturated fat, but it is mostly in the form of medium-chain saturated fatty acids (MCFAs), particularly lauric acid. MCFAs are used up more quickly by the body than other saturated fats and are less likely to be stored as fat.

1   Heat the stock in a saucepan with the coconut milk, chilli, mushrooms and lime leaves. Bring to the boil, then add the chicken and simmer for 10–15 minutes.

2   Using a slotted spoon, remove the chicken from the stock and set aside to cool slightly. When cool enough to handle, finely slice the chicken into bite-sized pieces.

3   Return the chicken to the stock and add the vegetables, fish sauce, sugar and lime juice. Cook for just a few more minutes, until the vegetables soften but still have a little bite.

4   Ladle into bowls and sprinkle over the chopped coriander to serve.

RICE, NOODLES, SUSHI & EGGS }

- 238 calories
- 0.7g saturated fat

Japanese-style rice with spring onion & ginger sauce

This fabulous rice dish is inspired by a recipe in David Chang's great book *Momofuku*. If you've never seen it, get your hands on one soon – it's kick-ass! You can use the sauce with everything from noodles and brown rice to salads and grilled chicken or fish.

Serves 4 as a side dish or small plate

100g peas, fresh or frozen

2 spring onions, thinly sliced

10g or 2cm fresh root ginger, grated

1 tbsp light oil, such as groundnut

2 tbsp ready-made sushi rice seasoning vinegar,
or make your own (*see* Tip, page 44)

1 quantity Easy Japanese-style Rice (*see* page 44)

salt

1   Cook the peas in boiling, salted water for 2–3 minutes, depending on whether they're fresh or frozen, then drain.

2   Put the spring onions, ginger, oil and sushi rice seasoning vinegar into a bowl or blender and mix well or blend briefly to make a sauce.

3   Stir the peas into the sauce, then fold into the rice.

- 270 calories
- trace saturated fat

Easy Japanese-style rice
Perfectly seasoned Japanese-style rice is really easy to make. All you need is a small saucepan with a lid, and a timer helps too. Use this delicious, seasoned, sticky rice for sushi, as a side dish, or as a base for the Grilled Chicken Teriyaki or Salmon Teriyaki (*see* pages 120 and 136). It freezes well too, so make a double quantity and keep the rest for another time. (The amounts below make 350g cooked rice.)

Serves 4 as a small plate

150g uncooked Japanese-style short-grain rice

180ml water, filtered if possible

3 tsp ready-made sushi rice seasoning vinegar, or make your own (*see* below)

1   Wash the rice in cold tap water until the water runs clear. This should take a couple of rinses. Drain and set aside for at least 15 minutes.

2   Put the rice into a saucepan and add the filtered water. Cover and bring to the boil (about 1–2 minutes), then reduce the heat and simmer for 12 minutes. Turn off the heat and leave, still covered, for 10 minutes.

3   Wet a flat tray and spread the rice over it. Sprinkle with the sushi rice seasoning vinegar and stir gently but thoroughly with a wooden spoon, lifting and folding the rice to help it cool slightly and absorb the seasoning. If you want to be really Japanese about it, you can fan it to help it cool.

Tip: Homemade sushi rice seasoning vinegar – although ready-made seasoning is widely available, it's easy to make your own. Simply mix together 1 teaspoon rice vinegar, 2 teaspoons mirin, ½ teaspoon sugar and ½ teaspoon salt. (These quantities make 3 teaspoons of seasoning, but can be multiplied proportionally to make as much as you like. If stored in a screwtop jar, the seasoning will keep for at least a month.

Variations: Pimp up a plain rice side dish with furikake or soy-toasted seeds (*see* page 89), or make our famously good spring onion and ginger sauce (*see* page 42).

- 141 calories
- 0.3g saturated fat

Brown rice for sushi As an even

healthier sushi option, try using brown rice. Unlike polished white rice, brown rice still contains all its valuable nutrients, giving us the full benefit of its fibre, vitamins and blood sugar stabilizing properties.

Serves 4 as a side dish or small plate

150g uncooked Japanese-style short-grain brown rice

200ml water, filtered if possible

3 tsp ready-made sushi rice seasoning vinegar, or make your own (see Tip, opposite)

1   Wash the rice in cold tap water until the water runs clear, then drain and set aside for at least 15 minutes.

2   Put the rice into a saucepan and add the filtered water. Cover and bring to the boil (about 1–2 minutes), then reduce the heat and simmer for 30 minutes. Turn off the heat and leave, still covered, for 10 minutes.

3   Wet a flat tray and spread the rice over it. Sprinkle with the sushi rice seasoning vinegar and stir gently but thoroughly with a wooden spoon, lifting and folding the rice to help it cool slightly and absorb the seasoning.

- 233 calories
- 2.6g saturated fat

Seven veg & brown rice potsu with ithai sauce

The base of brown and wild rice makes this recipe a great low-GI favourite to have at home or take to work – a deliciously filling yet tummy-light meal, bursting with nutrients. It's also packed with vitamins and antioxidants from the veg mixture, which counts as half of your five-a-day. Any leftovers will keep in the fridge for up to two days, and can be reheated for another meal, but remember that cooked rice should be reheated only once.

Serves 4

150g mixed brown and wild rice

1 large carrot, topped, tailed and cut into fine sticks

1 red pepper, cored, deseeded and sliced

1 leek, trimmed, cleaned and sliced

100g broccoli, broken into florets

100g or a handful of green beans, topped

100g or a handful of sugarsnap peas

100g or a handful of spinach

1 quantity ithai Sauce (see page 173)

salt

1 Wash the rice thoroughly and cover it with warm water. Set aside to soak for at least 10 minutes.

2 Bring a large pan of water to the boil, add a good pinch of salt and cook all the vegetables except for the spinach for 3 minutes. Add the spinach 30 seconds before the end of the cooking time.

3 Reserve the cooking water and, using a slotted spoon, transfer all the vegetables to a colander and set aside to drain, covering to keep warm.

4 Drain the rice, then add it to the vegetable water (which will now be full of nutrients) and boil it for 15 minutes, or according to the packet instructions. Drain well and divide between bowls. Spoon the warm vegetables on top and serve with ithai sauce.

»
- 300 calories
- 3.8g saturated fat

Grilled chicken & brown rice potsu with ithai sauce

Juicy pieces of grilled chicken on nutrient-packed brown rice plus a mountain of vegetables topped with itsu's famous ithai sauce – what could be better?

Serves 4

150g mixed brown and wild rice

150g boneless, skinless chicken thighs

1 tsp light oil, such as groundnut, for coating

1 large carrot, topped, tailed and cut into fine sticks

1 red pepper, cored, deseeded and sliced

100g or a handful of green beans, topped

100g or a handful of mangetout

100g or a handful of shiitake mushrooms, halved

100g or a handful of spinach

100g or a handful of bean sprouts

1 quantity ithai Sauce (*see* page 173)

salt and black pepper

1   Wash the rice thoroughly and cover with warm water. Set aside to soak for at least 10 minutes.

2   Heat the grill to its highest setting. Put the chicken thighs in a roasting tin, season well with salt and pepper and coat with the oil. Grill for 10 minutes, turning halfway through the cooking time. Remove and allow to cool slightly before cutting the chicken into pieces.

3   Meanwhile, bring a large pan of water to the boil, add a good pinch of salt and cook all the vegetables except for the spinach and bean sprouts for 3 minutes. Add the spinach and bean sprouts 30 seconds before the end of the cooking time. Drain well and cover to keep warm.

4   Drain the rice and add it to the vegetable water, which will now be full of nutrients, and boil for 15 minutes, or according to the packet instructions. Drain well.

5   Put the rice into serving bowls and top with the chicken pieces and vegetables. Pour ithai sauce over each one and serve with the remaining sauce on the side.

{ **Variations:** Try different vegetables, perhaps leeks, tenderstem broccoli or pak choi, with edamame (soya) beans. Furikake or sesame seeds, preferably toasted, or Toasted Pumpkin Seed Topping (*see* page 171) can be sprinkled on the finished dish to garnish, but just 1 tablespoon will add another 34 calories and 0.6g saturated fat to the whole dish.

- 299 calories
- 4.6g saturated fat

Grilled chicken & noodle potsu with dynamite broth

At itsu we top our potsus with pickled kombu, a dark green seaweed that gives them extra crunch. It is available from oriental food shops, but if you have difficulty getting hold of it, use pumpkin seeds or Pickled Cucumber with Ginger (*see* page 93). This yummy, healthy dinner dish is a great reason to keep some Dynamite Broth in the fridge.

Serves 4

200g boneless, skinless chicken thighs

½ tsp light oil, such as groundnut, for coating

1 large carrot, topped, tailed and cut into fine sticks

1 red pepper, cored, deseeded and sliced

100g or a handful of green beans, topped

100g or a handful of mangetout

100g or a handful of shiitake mushrooms, halved

100g or a handful of spinach

100g or a handful of bean sprouts

1 quantity Dynamite Broth (*see* page 23)

250g instant udon noodles or 150g dried udon noodles ....

salt and black pepper

2 tbsp furikake or sesame seeds, preferably toasted, or Toasted Pumpkin Seed Topping (*see* page 171), to garnish

1   Heat the grill to its highest setting. Put the chicken thighs in a roasting tin, season well with salt and pepper and coat with the oil. Grill for 10 minutes, turning halfway through the cooking time. Remove and allow to cool slightly before cutting the chicken into bite-sized pieces.

2   Meanwhile, bring a large pan of water to the boil, add a good pinch of salt and cook all the vegetables except for the spinach and bean sprouts for 3 minutes. Add the spinach and bean sprouts 30 seconds before the end of the cooking time. Drain well and cover to keep warm.

3   Heat the dynamite broth in a saucepan. Meanwhile, cook the noodles in boiling water according to the packet instructions. Drain and divide the noodles between serving bowls.

4   Put the vegetables and chicken on top of the noodles, then pour over the hot broth. Sprinkle furikake or sesame seeds, preferably toasted, or toasted pumpkin seed topping on top of each portion.

Tip: Several parts of this recipe can be prepared in advance. The noodles can be cooked and dressed with a little groundnut oil to prevent them from sticking together. The vegetable mixture can also be pre-cooked and stored in the fridge until needed. Warm through before just serving.

- 289 calories
- 3.6g saturated fat

Seven veg & udon potsu with dynamite broth

A mountain of vegetables on a bed of steaming noodles with our famous Dynamite Broth. Dried udon are slightly skinnier, have a firmer texture than other noodles, and store well.

Serves 4

1 large carrot, topped, tailed and cut into fine sticks

1 red pepper, cored, deseeded and sliced

100g or a handful of green beans, topped

100g or a handful of mangetout

100g or a handful of shiitake mushrooms, halved

100g or a handful of spinach

100g or a handful of bean sprouts

1 quantity Dynamite Broth (*see* page 23)

150g dried udon noodles or 200g instant udon noodles

salt

40g Toasted Pumpkin Seed Topping (*see* page 171), to garnish

1   Bring a large pan of water to the boil, add a good pinch of salt and cook all the vegetables except for the spinach and bean sprouts for 3 minutes. Add the spinach and bean sprouts for the last 30 seconds of the cooking time. Drain well and cover to keep warm.

2   Heat the dynamite broth in a saucepan.

3   Meanwhile, cook the noodles in boiling water according to the packet instructions.

4   Drain and divide the noodles between serving bowls. Put the vegetables on top and pour over the hot broth. Sprinkle with the toasted pumpkin seed topping to serve.

- 247 calories
- 1.1g saturated fat

Hot soba noodles in mushroom broth

A butterfly-light but flavour-filled broth full of nutrient-dense fresh and dried mushrooms and light soba noodles. Imagine a plate of pasta without the calories.

Serves 2

1 litre instant dashi, Homemade Dashi Stock (*see* page 165) or water

10g dried shiitake or any other strongly flavoured dried mushrooms

2 tbsp soy sauce

1 tsp rice vinegar

1 tbsp mirin

100g mixture of fresh mushrooms, sliced or cut into small pieces (eg shiitake, oyster, enoki or buna shimeji – all available from big supermarkets)

70g dried soba noodles

2 spring onions, finely chopped, to garnish

salt

Nutritional tip: Soba noodles are made from buckwheat flour, which is gluten-free and full of rutin, a bioflavanoid that extends the action of vitamin C and acts as an antioxidant. Buckwheat is also high in magnesium, which helps with energy production. These noodles will keep your blood sugar levels steadier than many other carbohydrates.

1   Pour the stock into a saucepan and bring to the boil. Add the dried mushrooms and simmer for 10 minutes.

2   Strain the stock, and chop the mushrooms finely. Return both to the pan and add the soy sauce, vinegar, mirin and fresh mushrooms. Simmer for 5 minutes.

3   Meanwhile, cook the noodles in boiling, salted water for 7 minutes, or according to the packet instructions. Drain and divide between 2 bowls. Ladle over the stock and mushrooms, then sprinkle with the spring onions to garnish.

Step-by-step sushi 'Sushi' is a general term used

to describe rice seasoned with vinegar and combined with other ingredients.

There are numerous styles and forms of sushi, but we've chosen just a few of the best to get you started.

Maki are rolled sushi – rice rolled around a filling with a sheet of nori on the outside (*hosomaki* or *futomaki*), or with nori rolled around the filling and rice on the outside of the roll (*uramaki*).

Nigiri are flattened sushi – small oblongs of hand-pressed rice with a topping laid over them.

Temaki or **hand rolls** are simple cone shapes. These are best made just before you eat them so that the nori stays crisp and holds its shape. They're great fun to make with a group of friends: just lay out all the ingredients and get everyone rolling their own.

Note: the Japanese don't use chopsticks to eat sushi – they pick the pieces up with their fingers.

How to make maki with rice inside The neat little rolls are

easy to master, consisting simply of a filling rolled inside a sheet of seaweed. You might like to practise with just rice at first in order to get the hang of the rolling technique.

TO MAKE 12 MAKI YOU WILL NEED

1 sheet of nori

100g or 2 small handfuls of cooked Easy Japanese-style Rice (*see* page 44)

your chosen filling (*see* pages 56–7 for inspiration)

1 Place the nori sheet on a work surface with the lines running vertically. Fold the sheet in half lengthways, then tear or cut along the fold so you have 2 rectangles.

2 Lay 1 rectangle on a sushi mat. Arrange the other ingredients around the mat, and place a bowl of warm water alongside. Wet your fingers in the water, then press half the rice over the nori, leaving a clear 1cm border along the top edge.

3 Arrange your chosen filling neatly on the rice along the edge nearest to you.

4 Lift the edge of the mat and roll it away from you using your thumbs whilst holding the filling in place with your fingers. Continue lifting the mat until the filled nori forms a roll underneath it. Dab a little water on the clear border of the nori and press to seal it. Chop the ends off to neaten and cut the finished roll into 6 equal pieces. Repeat this process with the remaining half sheet of nori.

- 196 calories
- 0.4g saturated fat

Spicy tuna fish maki
Finely chopped pickled ginger inside these little rice rolls gives them that extra-special zing.

Makes 12

1 sheet of nori

180g (about 2 handfuls) cooked Easy Japanese-style Rice (*see* page 44)

40g very fresh tuna, cut into long strips

2 tbsp ready-made pickled ginger, finely chopped

TO SERVE (OPTIONAL)

soy sauce

wasabi paste

1   Follow steps 1 and 2 on page 54.

2   Put a strip of tuna along the edge of the rice nearest you and cover with a layer of the pickled ginger.

3   Roll up the nori and cut into pieces as shown in step 4 on page 54.

4   Repeat all these steps with the remaining ingredients.

5   Serve with soy sauce and wasabi paste for dipping, if liked.

- 251 calories
- 2g saturated fat

Salmon & avocado maki An all-time
favourite at itsu, these fresh salmon, creamy avocado and crunchy cucumber rolls
are one of our best sellers.

Makes 12

1 sheet of nori

180g (about 2 handfuls) cooked Easy
Japanese-style Rice (*see* page 44)

40g very fresh salmon, cut into strips
6cm long

½ ripe avocado, thinly sliced

6 cucumber batons, about 9cm long
and 5mm wide, peeled and deseeded

TO SERVE (OPTIONAL)

soy sauce

wasabi paste

1   Follow steps 1 and 2 on page 54.

2   Put a strip of salmon along the edge of the rice nearest you and
cover with strips of avocado and cucumber.

3   Roll up the nori and cut into pieces as shown in step 4 on page 54.

4   Repeat all these steps with the remaining ingredients.

5   Serve with soy sauce and wasabi paste for dipping, if liked.

How to make maki with rice outside
We might describe this as an inside-out version of the previous maki because in this case the nori-covered filling is in the middle of the roll with the rice around the outside.

TO MAKE 12 MAKI YOU WILL NEED

1 sheet of nori

200g or 4 small handfuls of cooked Easy Japanese-style Rice (*see* page 44)

1 tbsp sesame seeds, preferably toasted

your chosen filling (*see* pages 60–1 for inspiration)

1 Place the nori sheet on a work surface with the lines running vertically. Fold the sheet in half lengthways, then tear or cut along the fold so you have 2 rectangles.

2 Lay 1 rectangle on a clean board. Arrange the other ingredients around it and place a bowl of warm water alongside. Wet your fingers in the water, then press half the rice over the nori. Sprinkle with half the sesame seeds.

3 Lay a sheet of cling film on a sushi mat. Lift the rice-covered nori sheet and place it rice-side down on the cling film. (Don't worry – the rice is sticky, so it won't fall off.) Add your chosen filling, placing it near to the edge of the nori closest to you.

4 Lift the edge of the mat and roll it away from you using your thumbs whilst holding the filling in place with your fingers. Continue lifting the mat and the cling film until the filled nori forms a roll underneath them. Dab a little water on the uncovered top edge of the nori to seal it. Chop the ends off to neaten and cut the finished roll into 6 equal pieces. Repeat this process with the remaining half sheet of nori.

- 287 calories
- 2.6g saturated fat

Crab California maki You need only a teeny bit
of crab for these rolls, so use any left over to make Crab Crystal Rolls (*see* page 157),
or eat it the next day on rice crackers with avocado and coriander as a yummy snack.

Makes 12

1 sheet of nori

about 200g cooked Easy Japanese-style Rice (*see* page 44)

about 1 tbsp sesame seeds, preferably toasted

4 tsp (about 20g) cooked crabmeat

½ ripe avocado, thinly sliced

12 chives

6 cucumber batons, about 9cm long and 5mm wide, peeled and deseeded

TO SERVE

soy sauce

wasabi paste

1   Follow steps 1–3 on page 58.

2   Put half the crab along the edge of the rice nearest you and cover with half the avocado, chives and cucumber.

3   Roll up and finish the maki as shown in step 4 on page 58.

4   Repeat all these steps with the remaining ingredients.

5   Serve with soy sauce and wasabi paste for dipping.

- 208 calories
- 1g saturated fat

Rainbow vegetable maki These maki

not only look pretty, but they're also suitable for vegetarians as they are fish-free.

Makes 12

1 sheet of nori

about 200g (4 small handfuls) cooked Easy Japanese-style Rice (*see* page 44)

about 1 tbsp sesame seeds, preferably toasted

8 raw fine green beans

½ ripe avocado, thinly sliced

12 chives

6 raw carrot sticks, about 9cm long and 5mm wide

1 tsp Spicy Sauce (*see* page 171, optional)

TO SERVE (OPTIONAL)

soy sauce

wasabi paste

1 Follow steps 1–3 on page 58.

2 Lay two pairs of green beans along the edge of the rice nearest you and cover with half of the avocado, chives and carrot.

3 Spread half the spicy sauce over the filling, if using.

4 Roll up and finish the maki as shown in step 4 on page 58.

5 Repeat all these steps with the remaining ingredients.

6 Serve with soy sauce and wasabi paste for dipping, if liked.

Variations: Vary the vegetables – try courgette or cooked squash – or even use soba noodles as a filling. The world is your oyster! Use furikake or linseed instead of sesame seeds.

How to make a hand roll

Easy-peasy temaki or hand rolls are a great introduction to making sushi. Roll them up and eat them straight away like ice-cream cones.

TO MAKE 2 HAND ROLLS YOU WILL NEED

1 sheet of nori

100g or 2 small handfuls of cooked Easy Japanese-style Rice (*see* page 44)

your chosen filling (*see* page 64 for inspiration)

1   Place the nori sheet on a clean board with the lines running vertically. Fold the sheet in half, then tear or cut along the fold so you have 2 rectangles.

2   Arrange the other ingredients around the nori and place a bowl of warm water alongside. Wet your fingers in the water, then press half the rice over the lower half of 1 nori rectangle.

3   Lay your chosen filling over the rice diagonally.

4   Lift the bottom left-hand corner and fold it towards the diagonally opposite corner of the rice to make a cone shape. Hold the narrowest point of the cone (middle left) and continue rolling tightly towards the top left of the nori. Dab a little water on the nori to seal the finished cone. Repeat steps 2–4 to make the second roll.

- 143 calories
- 2.1g saturated fat

Salmon hand rolls

Here's a chance to use the technique on page 62, this time with a salmon filling. Once you've got the hang of it, you could use any of the other sushi fillings as alternatives.

Makes 4

2 sheets of nori, cut in half lengthways (*see* page 62, step 1)

about 200g (4 small handfuls) cooked Easy Japanese-style Rice (*see* page 44)

½ tsp wasabi paste

4 cucumber batons, about 12cm long and 5mm wide, deseeded

150g skinned salmon fillet, chopped

½ avocado, sliced

1 tbsp fresh coriander leaves

4 tbsp tobiko (optional)

1 tbsp sesame seeds, preferably toasted, or furikake

1   Prepare all the ingredients and arrange them around a clean board. (Even better is to divide each ingredient into 4 piles ready to go into each roll.) Place a bowl of warm water alongside.

2   Wet your fingers, then press rice onto the nori as described on page 62, step 2. Dab the wasabi over the rice.

3   Place a cucumber stick diagonally across the rice from the top left corner. Put a quarter of the salmon, avocado, coriander and tobiko (if using) on top, then sprinkle with sesame seeds.

4   Roll the nori carefully to make a cone shape as described on page 62, step 4.

5   Repeat, using the rest of the ingredients to make 3 more cones.

Nutritional tip: Nori is rich in vitamins, and the delicious flavour makes it great to use as a savoury wrapping.

Salmon sushi

You don't have to be a sushi master to make these flattened sushi, known as nigiri: you don't even need a sushi mat. All that's required is some super-fresh fish and a bowl of rice, and off you go!

Makes 6

80g very fresh salmon fillet, skinned and cut into 6 thin slices

wasabi paste

80g cooked Easy Japanese-style Rice (see page 44)

TO SERVE

soy sauce

ready-made pickled ginger

1 Prepare all the ingredients and arrange them around a clean board. Place a bowl of warm water alongside.

2 Lay a slice of salmon in the palm of one hand and spread a dab of wasabi over it.

3 Wet your fingers in the bowl of water, then take a large pinch of the rice and press it onto the salmon.

4 Put your index finger and ring finger on either side of the rice and your middle finger on top and gently press to shape it into a long rectangle. Squeeze the ends to neaten them.

5 Put the sushi on a plate and repeat with the rest of the fish and rice.

6 Serve with soy sauce and pickled ginger.

{ Variations: Try using sea bass, tuna or sliced scallops instead of salmon.

- 92 calories
- 0.1g saturated fat

Cooked prawn sushi These nigiri are great for kids and for pregnant women who can't eat raw fish.

Serves 2

6 large cooked peeled prawns (about 60g), tails left on

80g cooked Easy Japanese-style Rice (*see* page 44)

wasabi paste

TO SERVE

soy sauce

ready-made pickled ginger

1 Prepare all the ingredients and arrange them around a clean board. Place a bowl of warm water alongside.

2 Score the underside of each prawn so that it uncurls and can be pressed flat. Place a prawn in the palm of one hand and spread a dab of wasabi over the underside.

3 Wet your fingers in the bowl of water, then take a large pinch of the rice and press it over the wasabi.

4 Put your index finger and ring finger on either side of the rice and your middle finger on top and gently press to shape it into a long rectangle. Squeeze the ends to neaten them.

5 Transfer to a plate, prawn side up, and repeat the steps with the remaining ingredients. Serve with soy sauce and pickled ginger.

- 244 calories
- 3.6g saturated fat

Scrambled eggs with prawns & nori

Here's something easy and healthy to throw together for a quick supper or when time is short. It's light but filling, tasty and full of nutrients.

Serves 2

1 tsp light oil, such as groundnut, for frying

100g cooked or raw peeled prawns, tails discarded

4 spring onions, sliced

4 free-range eggs

3 tbsp soy sauce

1 sheet of nori, cut into fine strips (scissors are best for this)

1   Heat a frying pan, add the oil, then stir-fry the prawns and spring onions for a couple of minutes until the prawns start to colour.

2   Whisk the eggs and soy sauce together and pour into the pan. Lower the heat and cook, stirring and folding, for a couple of minutes until the eggs are just set but still a little creamy.

3   Sprinkle over the nori and stir once more. Spoon onto plates and serve straight away, while the texture is just right.

- 198 calories
- 3.6g saturated fat

Japanese omelette
A perfect skinny and speedy solution for busy days, this omelette is easy to make and bursting with flavour. Eggs, always free-range, frequently feature on itsu's menu because they are high in protein and nutrients, and low in calories.

Serves 2

4 free-range eggs

1 tbsp mirin

1 tbsp soy sauce

1 tsp chopped chives, plus a few extra for garnish

1 tsp bonito flakes (optional)

1 tsp light oil, such as groundnut, for frying

soy sauce, for dipping (optional)

chives, to garnish

1   Crack the eggs into a bowl. Add the mirin, soy sauce, chives and bonito flakes (if using) and whisk well.

2   Heat a frying pan, add the oil and use a piece of kitchen paper to spread it around the pan and remove any excess.

3   Pour a ladleful of the egg mixture into the pan and tilt gently so that it coats the bottom. Cook for a few seconds, until it starts to set. Using a palette knife or spatula, lift one side of the omelette and roll or fold it towards one end of the pan.

4   Leaving the rolled omelette in the pan, pour in another ladleful of the egg mixture, lifting the first roll so that the uncooked egg flows underneath it. Cook for a few seconds until slightly set, then roll or fold it back over the thin layer of egg like the first omelette. Repeat this process until all the mixture is used up.

5   Transfer to a board and cut into thick pieces so you can see all the layers. Serve with soy sauce for dipping, if desired, and garnish with chives. Alternatively, allow to cool, then wrap the roll to eat cold as a healthy snack on the run.

VEGETABLES
& SALADS }

- 285 calories (plus 160 calories if eaten in flatbread)
- 2.6g saturated fat (plus 0.3g if eaten in flatbread)

Baked salmon in miso

Juicy salmon flaked over a bed of healthy vegetables and dressed with a creamy, herby sauce. This can be eaten as a slimming salad or in a warmed flatbread for a delicious, portable lunch. (If you go for the flatbread option, flake the salmon over the other ingredients.)

Serves 2

2 skinned salmon fillets, about 100g each

large handful of green beans, topped

large handful of sugarsnap peas or mangetout

small handful of edamame (soya) beans

2 handfuls of salad leaves, plus grated carrot or chopped radishes for extra crunch (optional)

3 tsp Herb Dressing (*see* page 166)

flatbreads or pitta breads, to serve (optional)

2 tsp furikake, or sesame seeds, preferably toasted, or Toasted Pumpkin Seed Topping (*see* page 171)

MARINADE

2 tbsp miso paste

1 tsp water

1 tsp soy sauce

1 Preheat the oven to 200°C/fan 180°C/gas mark 6.

2 Meanwhile, make the marinade by combining all the ingredients for it in a bowl.

3 Place two A4 pieces of foil on a work surface and lay a salmon fillet on each. Cover both sides of the salmon with the marinade and wrap loosely in the foil. Place in a roasting tin and bake for 8–10 minutes (a tail fillet will take less time than a thicker fillet).

4 Steam or boil the green beans, sugarsnap peas or mangetout and edamame beans for 3 minutes.

5 Dress the salad leaves, plus the carrot or radishes (if using), with the herb dressing.

6 Arrange the salad, vegetables and salmon on 2 flatbreads or pitta breads, sprinkle with the toasted seeds and then roll up. Alternatively, divide the salad between 2 plates, top with the vegetables, place the salmon alongside and sprinkle with the toasted seeds to finish.

{ **Nutritional tip:** Just 1 tablespoon of sesame seeds provides around one-tenth of your daily requirement of calcium and magnesium

- 131 calories (plus 160 calories if eaten in flatbread)
- 1.5g saturated fat (plus 0.3g if eaten in flatbread)

Super low-calorie smoked chicken salad

This is the skinniest option in our salad or sandwich range. Quick to assemble and super-healthy to eat, it's packed with protein from the chicken and edamame.

Serves 2

150g smoked chicken breast, sliced

2 tbsp Spicy Sauce (*see* page 171)

100g edamame (soya) beans or green beans, topped

100g mixed salad leaves

4 tbsp Herb Dressing (*see* page 166)

flatbreads or pitta breads, to serve (optional)

1 tbsp chopped chives

salt

Variations: Ordinary grilled chicken breast can be used instead of smoked chicken. For extra protein, add a hard-boiled egg.

1   Dress the sliced chicken breast with the spicy sauce.

2   Cook the beans in boiling, salted water for 3 minutes. Drain and refresh under cold water.

3   Dress the salad leaves and beans with the herb dressing. Arrange on 2 flatbreads or pitta breads, put the chicken on top, sprinkle with the chives and then roll up. Alternatively, divide the dressed salad between 2 plates, top with the chicken and sprinkle with the chives to finish.

Top: Hip & humble houmous salad (*see* page 80);
Bottom: Tangy tuna with spicy sauce

» • 219 calories (plus 160 calories if eaten in flatbread)
• 1.4g saturated fat (plus 0.3g if eaten in flatbread)

Tangy tuna with spicy sauce

Tuna is a 'meaty' fish, so it's great for filling you up without being too calorific. The pickled ginger and the spicy sauce give it a wonderful tang, making a simple ingredient taste deliciously more-ish.

Serves 2

100g edamame (soya) beans, peas or broad beans

150g canned tuna in brine, drained

1 tbsp ready-made pickled ginger, finely chopped, or 10g (2cm) fresh root ginger, grated

1 tbsp coriander, chopped

1 tbsp chives, chopped

3 tbsp Spicy Sauce (*see* page 171)

handful of mixed salad leaves

1 carrot, cut into fine sticks

2 tbsp Herb Dressing or Asian Pesto (*see* page 166)

salt

flatbreads or pitta breads, to serve (optional)

1 Cook the beans or peas in boiling, salted water for 3 minutes. Drain and refresh under cold water.

2 Mix the tuna with the ginger, coriander, chives, spicy sauce and a pinch of salt.

3 Combine the salad leaves with the carrots and dress with the herb dressing or Asian pesto (if you prefer, the dressing can be offered separately). Arrange the salad on a plate and place the beans and tuna mixture on top. Alternatively, place inside 2 flatbreads or pitta breads and roll up.

Variations: Serve on a bed of rice, or with a hard-boiled egg for extra protein. The tangy tuna can also be used as a filling for maki (*see* pages 54 and 58).

Tip: When using canned tuna, always check its sustainability. Sainsbury's, Marks & Spencer and Waitrose rate high in the Greenpeace league table.

»
- 291 calories (plus 160 calories if eaten in flatbread)
- 2g saturated fat (plus 0.3g if eaten in flatbread)

Hip & humble houmous salad

Spicy, herby houmous on a bed of salad topped with crunchy seeds is a protein-packed plateful, but makes a great sandwich filling too. It's also a good dip to eat with carrot, cucumber and celery sticks for a healthy snack.

Serves 2

150g reduced-fat ready-made houmous

1 tbsp Sriracha chilli sauce or 1 tsp chilli flakes

1 tbsp chopped chives

1 tbsp chopped coriander

100g or large handful of edamame (soya) beans

2 handfuls of mixed salad leaves

1 carrot, cut into fine sticks

small handful of cherry tomatoes

salt

15g Toasted Pumpkin Seed Topping, to garnish (*see* page 171)

flatbread or pitta bread, to serve (optional)

1   Mix the houmous with the chilli sauce and herbs.

2   Cook the edamame beans in boiling, salted water for 3 minutes, then drain and refresh under cold water.

3   Arrange the salad leaves, carrot and tomatoes on small plates, sprinkle over the edamame beans and spoon the houmous on top. Sprinkle with the toasted pumpkin seed topping and serve. Alternatively, place inside a flatbread and roll up.

Nutritional tip: Pumpkin seeds are full of zinc and omega-3.

Beef salad with green beans & lime marinade

This Asian-inspired salad is crunchy, juicy and zesty. Poaching the beef in water is healthier than frying it and makes it easier not to overcook. It's also a great way to use the leftovers from a Sunday roast.

Serves 2

100g beef fillet, such as sirloin, rump or skirt, sliced very thinly

100g or handful of green beans, topped, or mangetout, or 50/50 mixture

100g or handful of spinach leaves

100g or handful of bean sprouts

2 shallots, chopped

large mixed handful of basil, coriander and mint, roughly chopped

1 tbsp roasted salted peanuts, chopped

salt

MARINADE

2–3 tbsp lime juice

1 tsp palm sugar or brown sugar alternative

1 garlic clove, grated or crushed

2 tbsp fish sauce

½ hot red Thai chilli, chopped

1 First make the marinade by combining all the ingredients in a bowl.

2 Put the beef in a bowl, pour boiling water over it and leave for 30 seconds. Drain and return the beef to the bowl, cover with the marinade and set aside.

3 Cook the beans or mangetout in salted boiling water for 2 minutes. Drain and refresh under cold water. Mix with the spinach, bean sprouts, shallots and herbs, then combine with the beef and marinade. Sprinkle with the chopped peanuts and serve.

- 172 calories (plus 56 calories if peanuts included)
- 0.6g saturated fat (plus 0.8g if peanuts included)

Vietnamese chicken salad itsu made

the mistake of taking this lettuce-free salad off the menu last year. Customer demand ensured its permanent return two days later. The combination of crunchy vegetables, juicy chicken and fine noodles in a sweet, hot, salty dressing topped with crunchy peanuts is authentically Vietnamese, and it tastes as good as it looks. If you want to keep the second portion for lunch or dinner the next day, add the dressing just before eating.

Serves 2

15g thin glass noodles

100g cooked chicken breast, shredded into small pieces

½ shallot, finely sliced

¼ head of Chinese leaves or white cabbage, finely sliced

large handful of bean sprouts

1 carrot, grated or cut into fine sticks

2 mixed handfuls of coriander, basil and mint, roughly chopped

2 tbsp peanuts, roughly chopped (optional)

1 quantity Sweet Chilli Sauce (see page 167)

1   Put the noodles in a bowl and cover with boiling water for 3–5 minutes, or according to the packet instructions. Drain and refresh under cold water, then set aside.

2   Place all the remaining ingredients, apart from the sauce, in a large bowl and mix well. Add the noodles, gently untangling the strands as you go.

3   Pour the sauce over the salad and toss well before serving.

Variation: Try making this with prawns instead of chicken – a delicious (and still skinny) alternative.

»
- 174 calories
- 1.4g saturated fat

itsu's special salad
Packed with goodness and dressed with our special spicy sauce, this salad is so healthy that you will want to eat it with everything. It keeps well, so can be made in advance, and is perfect as a portable lunch.

Serves 2 as a main course, or 4 as a starter

25g thin glass noodles

100g edamame (soya) beans

large pinch of dried wakame

2 carrots, grated, or shaved into strips with a potato peeler ....

20g mixture of coriander, basil and mint, chopped

20g rocket leaves

10g pumpkin seeds

2 tsp sesame seeds, preferably toasted

100g firm tofu, cut into cubes

2 tbsp Spicy Sauce (see page 171)

> **Nutritional tips:** Carrots are a great source of vitamin A, which is important for a healthy immune system; edamame (soya) beans and tofu both contain high-quality protein and help to maintain a healthy hormone balance.

1 Put the noodles in a bowl and cover with boiling water for 3–5 minutes, or according to the packet instructions. Drain and refresh under cold water, then set aside.

2 Cook the edamame beans in boiling water for 3 minutes, then drain and refresh under cold water.

3 Soak the wakame in cold water for 5 minutes, then drain.

4 Put the noodles into a bowl, add the wakame, carrots, herbs, rocket, seeds, tofu and beans and toss together.

5 Serve the salad with the spicy sauce.

- 87 calories (plus 34 calories if sesame seeds included)
- 0.4g saturated fat (plus 0.6g if sesame seeds included)

Crisp salad with sesame dressing

Salads should be fun, easy and creative, and this colourful mixture of vegetables with creamy sesame sauce fits the bill. It makes a great portable lunch, and is a good way to use up whatever you have in the fridge, but try to use ingredients that retain their crunch, such as carrots, radishes, celery and peppers.

Serves 2

100g mixed salad leaves

1 carrot, grated or cut into fine sticks

1 red or green pepper, cored, deseeded and sliced

1 celery stick, sliced

small handful of radishes, halved

3 tbsp Sesame Sauce (*see* page 168)

1 tbsp sesame seeds, preferably toasted, to serve (optional)

1   Put all the ingredients (apart from the sauce and the seeds) into a bowl. Add the sesame sauce and mix well. Sprinkle with sesame seeds, if using, and serve.

Chopped salad with tofu, wakame & miso dressing

Here's a great way to use up any vegetables you might have lingering in the fridge, such as celery, carrots and bean sprouts. The creamy dressing turns them into something really special.

Serves 2

½ cucumber, cut into small cubes

small handful of cherry tomatoes, halved

½ green pepper, cored, deseeded and finely chopped

small handful of radishes, halved

1 spring onion, sliced

100g firm tofu, cut into cubes

2 tbsp dried wakame, soaked in cold water for 5 minutes then drained

1 quantity Miso Dressing (*see* page 168)

1 tsp sesame oil

1 tbsp sesame seeds, preferably toasted, to serve

1 Put all the vegetables into a bowl with the tofu and wakame. Add the dressing and sesame oil and mix gently. Serve with sesame seeds scattered over the top.

Tip: At itsu you'll find wakame in various soups and salads. To prepare it for use, all you need to do is soak the dried leaves in cold water for a few minutes to reconstitute it.

Nutritional tip: Apart from tasting delicious, wakame contains something called fucoxanthin, which can help burn fatty deposits.

Carrot & bean salad with toasted seeds

A colourful salad with plenty of crunch, this can be eaten as a small dish, or alongside a main course, such as Grilled Chicken Teriyaki (*see* page 120). If you haven't tried the shallot dressing before, you're in for a treat, and this recipe is a great excuse to make a jar of it to keep in the fridge.

Serves 2

150g green beans, topped

100g edamame (soya) beans

20g mixed pumpkin and sunflower seeds

1 tbsp soy sauce

150g carrots, shaved into strips with a potato peeler

1–2 tbsp Shallot Dressing (*see* page 172)

salt

1 Cook the green beans and edamame in boiling, salted water for 2 minutes. Drain and refresh under cold water.

2 Heat a dry frying pan. Cook the seeds, tossing occasionally, for about 1 minute, or until they start to toast. Pour over the soy sauce and turn off the heat. It will bubble and evaporate to form a dark, salty coating over the seeds, a bit like a peanut brittle.

3 Put the carrots, green beans and edamame into a bowl and mix well with the dressing. Serve with the toasted seeds sprinkled over the top.

- 242 calories
- 1.1g saturated fat

Soba noodle salad
Soft noodles and crunchy vegetables with a kick of chilli make this a filling but healthy salad. It's delicious with sesame seeds sprinkled over at the end.

Serves 2

90g soba noodles

4 tbsp Sesame Sauce (*see* page 168)

10g or 2cm fresh root ginger, grated

1 hot red Thai chilli, deseeded and chopped

small handful of coriander, chopped

¼ cucumber, chopped

2 spring onions, sliced

100g radishes, sliced

salt

1 tbsp sesame seeds, preferably toasted, to serve

Nutritional tip: Tahini (sesame seed paste), a constituent of the sesame sauce, contains vitamin E, an important antioxidant, which protects against cell damage.

1   Cook the soba noodles in 1.5 litres of boiling, salted water for 7 minutes. Drain and refresh under cold water. Set aside to cool.

2   Put the cold noodles into a bowl, add the sesame sauce and all the remaining ingredients, except for the sesame seeds, and mix well.

3   Divide the salad between 2 plates and sprinkle with the sesame seeds to serve.

- 26 calories
- trace saturated fat

Pickled cucumber with ginger

This simple, quick pickle tastes great with everything. Try it as a topping for a potsu, with rice or noodles, or added to a salad. It's also good as part of a bento box-style meal, with some Mackerel with Sweet Mirin Sauce (*see* page 154). It's hard to believe that something so tasty is this skinny, plus a portion counts as one of your five-a-day.

Serves 4

2 tbsp soy sauce

2 tbsp rice vinegar

1–2 tsp sugar or sugar alternative

½ cucumber, peeled and cut in half lengthways

10g or 2 cm fresh root ginger, thinly sliced

Variations: Other good vegetables to pickle include carrots, fennel, celery and radishes.

1   Mix the soy sauce, vinegar and sugar together in a bowl.

2   Using a teaspoon, scrape out and discard the cucumber seeds. Cut the flesh into thin slices.

3   Cut the ginger slices into narrow strips.

4   Add both the cucumber and the ginger to the soy mixture and chill for at least 30 minutes before eating.

- 134 calories
- 1.2g saturated fat

Spinach balls with sesame sauce

Spinach is a superfood packed with iron, folic acid and vitamin A. The sesame sauce makes it even more nutritious, being an excellent source of essential fats, magnesium and calcium.

Serves 2

400g spinach ....

3 tbsp Sesame Sauce (*see* page 168)

2 tsp sesame seeds, preferably toasted, to serve

Variation: Watercress can be used instead of spinach, and contains even more iron.

1   Cook the spinach in plenty of boiling water for 1–2 minutes, until fully wilted. Drain and refresh under cold water, then use your hands to squeeze it as dry as possible.

2   Divide the spinach in half and shape into two balls. Serve with the sesame sauce poured over the top, and sprinkle with the sesame seeds for extra crunch.

- 101 calories
- 1.4g saturated fat

Cucumber, sesame & spring onion salad

Fresh, light and bright, this salad is a great addition to all sorts of dishes. Try it with Chicken and Leek Yakitori or Salmon Teriyaki (*see* pages 116 or 136).

Serves 2

½ cucumber, deseeded and sliced into sticks

2 small spring onions, sliced

2 tsp rice vinegar

1 tsp mirin

1 tbsp sesame oil

½ hot red Thai chilli, chopped

pinch of salt

1 tbsp chopped coriander

1 tbsp sesame seeds, preferably toasted

1 Arrange the cucumber sticks on a plate and scatter the spring onion over the top.

2 Combine the vinegar, mirin, sesame oil, chilli and salt and pour the mixture over the cucumber. Sprinkle with the chopped coriander and sesame seeds before serving.

Nutritional tip: Just 5cm of cucumber counts as one of your five-a-day.

- 275 calories (plus 22 calories with sesame seeds)
- 2.7g saturated fat (plus 0.4g saturated fat with sesame seeds)

Tenderstem broccoli with sesame sauce

While delicious served warm, this dish can also be eaten cold, perhaps as part of a summer picnic. Sesame sauce is a favourite at itsu and goes beautifully with all sorts of freshly steamed or boiled leafy greens and beans.

Serves 2

200g tenderstem broccoli florets ....

1 quantity Sesame Sauce (*see* page 168)

2 tsp sesame seeds, preferably toasted, to serve (optional)

1   Steam the broccoli for 3 minutes, or cook in boiling water for 2 minutes, until just tender. Drain if necessary, and transfer to a plate.

2   Pour the sesame sauce over the broccoli and sprinkle with sesame seeds, if using, to serve.

Nutritional tip: Gently steaming vegetables preserves more of their nutrients and allows you to get the full benefit of their antioxidants, folic acid and fibre.

- 63 calories
- 0.6g saturated fat

Not-too-spicy broccoli

A popular dish served at itsu, this broccoli can also be eaten with your fingers for a healthy, skinny snack or try it as an accompaniment to Seared Miso-marinated Steak (*see* page 127).

Serves 2

200g tenderstem broccoli

1 tsp light oil, such as groundnut, for frying

1 hot red Thai chilli, deseeded and chopped

1 garlic clove, grated or crushed

20g or 4cm fresh root ginger, grated

1 tbsp soy sauce

flaked salt, to serve

1   Steam the broccoli for 3 minutes, or cook in boiling water for 2 minutes, until just tender. Drain if necessary, and transfer to a plate.

2   Heat a wok or deep frying pan and add the oil. Fry the chilli, garlic and ginger for 1 minute, stirring well. Add the cooked broccoli and soy sauce and toss to mix.

3   Serve the hot broccoli and sauce with salt flakes scattered on top.

- 249 calories
- 4.4g saturated fat

Tomato, tofu & avocado salad with yuzu-style dressing

This is itsu's dairy-free version of tomato and mozzarella salad – but it's healthier and skinnier than the Italian classic. Serve at room temperature for the best flavour.

Serves 2

1 ripe avocado, stoned and sliced

200g small sweet tomatoes or cherry tomatoes, halved

60g (about 6 tbsp) soft/silken tofu, broken into pieces

2 tbsp basil and mint leaves

½ quantity Yuzu-style Dressing (*see* page 170)

black pepper

1 Arrange the avocado and tomatoes on a serving plate.

2 Drop the tofu pieces over the top and sprinkle with the herbs and black pepper.

3 Pour over the dressing before serving.

Nutritional tip: Avocados are a rich source of vitamin E, which protects cells from damage.

- 96 calories (plus 34 calories if sesame seeds included)
- 0.4g saturated fat (plus 0.6g if sesame seeds included)

Baked aubergine with miso

Miso is a staple in Japanese cooking and an incredibly versatile ingredient in the kitchen. It's now recognised as an umami seasoning – something that adds a depth of flavour to dishes without itself being identifiable. This dish is delicious served hot with rice, or eaten at room temperature the next day.

Serves 2

1 aubergine, cut into 1cm slices

1 tsp light oil, such as groundnut, for greasing

small bunch of coriander, chopped

1 tbsp sesame seeds, preferably toasted, to sprinkle (optional)

SAUCE

1½ tbsp miso

2 tbsp mirin

1 tbsp sake

10g or 2cm fresh root ginger, grated

2 spring onions, sliced

1   Preheat the oven to 200°C/fan 180°C/gas mark 6.

2   To make the sauce, mix the miso, mirin and sake together in a large bowl to make a smooth paste. Stir in the ginger and onions.

3   Add the aubergine slices to the bowl and coat well with the sauce.

4   Grease a roasting tray with the oil and arrange the aubergine slices on it in a single layer so that they cook evenly. Bake for 20 minutes, or until soft and slightly brown. If the aubergine looks a little dry, add a splash of water.

5   Serve sprinkled with the coriander, plus the sesame seeds if you want some extra crunch.

- 238 calories (plus 34 calories if sesame seeds included; nori negligible)
- 2.2g saturated fat (plus 0.6g if sesame seeds included; nori 0g)

Grilled asparagus with miso hollandaise & poached egg

The Japanese diet contains relatively little dairy produce, but still includes the occasional rich sauce. Miso hollandaise is made without butter, but has all the creamy richness of the French classic. For a more substantial meal, serve the asparagus on a bed of Japanese-style rice as a vegetarian main course.

Serves 2

300g asparagus

2 tsp light oil, such as groundnut, for drizzling

pinch of salt

2 free-range eggs

1 tbsp furikake or sesame seeds, preferably toasted, and/or shredded nori, to serve (optional)

1 quantity Miso Hollandaise (*see* page 170)

black pepper

Nutritional tip: Asparagus is packed with even more folic acid than broccoli.

Variation: The dish can be made with other seasonal vegetables, such as tenderstem broccoli, carrots and baby leeks.

1   Heat the grill to its highest setting.

2   Snap off and discard the woody ends of the asparagus. Lay the asparagus on a baking sheet and drizzle the oil over it. Sprinkle with the salt and toss well to coat.

3   Grill for 8 minutes, checking the spears halfway through the cooking time and giving them a shake so they cook evenly.

4   Poach the eggs in boiling water for 3 minutes so that the white is set but the yolk runny.

5   Place the asparagus on serving plates and put an egg on top of each serving. Sprinkle with the seeds and/or nori (if using), season with black pepper and offer the miso hollandaise alongside.

VEGETABLES & SALADS

- 189 calories
- 2g saturated fat

Fried tofu with spicy teriyaki & salad

Warm pieces of tofu coated in a tangy ginger sauce served on a bed of salad make this a skinny but filling dish. It's an excellent vegetarian option, too, because it's full of 'good' protein from the tofu.

Serves 1 as a main course or 2 as a starter

100g firm tofu, sliced in half

1 tsp light oil, such as groundnut, for frying

large handful of mixed salad leaves

large handful of bean sprouts

small handful of cherry tomatoes, halved

1 tbsp furikake or sesame seeds, preferably toasted, or pumpkin seeds, or a mixture of all three

DRESSING

2 tbsp Teriyaki & Ginger Sauce (*see* page 169)

1 tsp Sriracha chilli sauce

1 tbsp sesame oil

1   Put the tofu slices on a plate and dab with kitchen paper to dry.

2   Heat a nonstick frying pan until really hot. Add the oil, then fry the tofu for a minute on each side, until golden brown. Remove from the pan and allow to cool slightly before cutting into large cubes.

3   Make the dressing by putting all the ingredients into a small bowl and mixing well.

4   Put the salad leaves, bean sprouts and tomatoes on plates and lay the tofu pieces on top. Drizzle with the dressing and sprinkle on the seeds to serve.

Nutritional tip: Bean sprouts contain iron, which is good for the blood. For extra antioxidants, sprinkle the finished dish with pomegranate seeds. (The seeds from half a pomegranate, shared between 2 plates, would add an extra 15 calories per person, but no more saturated fat.)

- 151 calories
- 1g saturated fat

Spicy hot edamame beans

This is a great snack to pile into a bowl and share; simply cook the pods whole, then pull them through your teeth to pop out the little green beans hidden inside. Steaming rather than boiling the beans locks in maximum nutrients. A simple bamboo steamer is great for this, but it's not essential.

Serves 2 as a starter or 4 as a snack

200g edamame (soya) beans in their pods

1 tsp light oil, such as groundnut, for frying

1 hot red Thai chilli, chopped

1 garlic clove, grated or crushed

20g or 4cm fresh root ginger, finely chopped

1 tbsp soy sauce

flaked salt, to serve (optional)

1   Steam the edamame for 3 minutes, or cook them in boiling water for 2 minutes. Drain well.

2   Heat a wok or deep frying pan and add the oil. Fry the chilli, garlic and ginger for about 1 minute, stirring well. Add the cooked pods and soy sauce and toss to mix.

3   Transfer to a bowl and serve the hot edamame pods and sauce, sprinkled with salt flakes if you wish.

- 274 calories
- 1.1g saturated fat

Vegetable tempura Here's a fun and easy way

to prepare any seasonal vegetables. The secret to crisp, light tempura batter is to get the oil hot enough and fry only small batches at a time. The hotter the oil, the less it is absorbed by the batter, and the healthier the result. Increase the quantities below and serve the tempura with ponzu sauce for a fabulous party snack. Note that the cooking oil can be reused; just cool and strain it, then store it in an airtight container.

Serves 2

1 small aubergine (about 300g)

200g asparagus

8 small spring onions, trimmed

100g green beans, topped

about 800ml sunflower oil, for deep-frying

1 quantity Ponzu Sauce (*see* page 169), to serve

BATTER

100g plain flour

25g cornflour

1 tsp baking powder

½ tsp salt

200–250ml chilled sparkling water

1 Cut the aubergine in half lengthways and then into 5mm crescents.

2 Snap off and discard the woody ends of the asparagus. Slice the remainder in half lengthways and then into short fingers.

3 Cut the spring onions into short fingers.

4 To make the batter, sift the flours and baking powder into a bowl and stir in the salt. Whisk in the water to make a smooth batter that has the consistency of pouring cream. Add more water if necessary.

5 In a deep saucepan, heat the oil to 180°C, or until a teaspoon of batter added to the pan sizzles and starts to brown immediately.

6 Warm a plate and cover it with kitchen paper.

7 Dip a handful of cut vegetables into the batter, then carefully lower them one at a time into the hot oil. Fry for less than a minute, until the batter is puffy and golden. Using tongs, transfer them to the prepared plate. Repeat until all the vegetables are cooked.

8 Serve the tempura hot, with the ponzu sauce in a bowl for dipping.

- 132 calories
- 0.2g saturated fat

Pickled vegetables with seaweed & edamame

Japanese sea vegetables are treasured ingredients – low in fat and beautifully varied in colour, texture and flavour. You can buy them dried in packets, so they store well and take just a few minutes to prepare. Alternatively, if you can't buy them, just use wakame – you'll still get all those wonderful sea nutrients.

Serves 2

handful of dried sea vegetables (available online or from good Japanese suppliers – *see* page 188)

50g edamame (soya) beans, fresh or frozen

1 carrot, shaved into thin strips using a potato peeler

1 celery stick, sliced

small handful of radishes, quartered

20g or 4cm fresh root ginger, or 1 tbsp ready-made pickled ginger, sliced

PICKLING SAUCE

3 tbsp mirin

3 tbsp rice vinegar

1 tsp sugar or sugar alternative

1 tsp salt

1 Put the dried sea vegetables into a bowl of warm water and leave to soak for 10 minutes.

2 Meanwhile, make the pickling sauce. Heat the mirin in a pan until it starts to boil. Add the remaining sauce ingredients and cook for 1 minute, until the sugar and salt have dissolved. Pour into a large bowl and allow to cool.

3 If using fresh edamame beans, cook them for 3 minutes in boiling water; if using frozen, just pour boiling water over them and leave for 3 minutes. Drain and refresh under cold water.

4 Drain the sea vegetables and add them with all the other vegetables and the ginger to the pickling sauce. Mix well, then cover and refrigerate for up to 24 hours, but for at least 15 minutes.

5 Serve straight away for a fresh crunchy texture, or leave in the fridge until needed.

MEAT }

- 182 calories
- 3g saturated fat

Mini Thai pork burgers
These neat little burgers, which you can eat with your fingers, are great for a picnic, an easy starter or as party snacks. Serve with sweet chilli sauce for dipping.

Serves 4

200g minced pork

½ lemon grass stalk, finely chopped

2 lime leaves, shredded

½ garlic clove, grated or crushed

10g or 2cm fresh root ginger, grated

1 hot red Thai chilli, finely chopped

zest of ½ lime

small bunch of coriander, chopped, plus extra sprigs to garnish

½ tsp salt

1 free-range egg, whisked

flour, for dusting

1 tbsp light oil, such as groundnut, for frying

1 quantity Sweet Chilli Sauce (see page 167)

black pepper

1   Put the minced pork into a bowl and add the lemon grass, lime leaves, garlic, ginger, chilli, lime zest, coriander and salt. Season with black pepper and, using a spoon, or your hands, mix together thoroughly.

2   Pour in half the whisked egg to bring the mixture together, adding the remainder if the mixture seems a little dry.

3   Form the mixture into 12 little balls, then flatten them into fat discs. Put them on a plate and refrigerate for 10 minutes.

4   Sprinkle some flour on a saucer and season with salt and pepper. Dust the burgers on both sides with the seasoned flour.

5   Heat a large frying pan and add the oil. Fry the burgers 4–6 at a time, depending on the size of your pan, for 3–4 minutes on each side. Transfer the cooked burgers to a warm plate and cook the remaining burgers in the same way.

6   Serve the burgers garnished with coriander sprigs with the sweet chilli sauce for dipping.

- 271 calories (plus 5 calories if sake used in sauce)
- 2.1g saturated fat

Chicken & leek yakitori

Yakitori means literally 'skewered chicken'. It's really easy to make under the grill, but even better on a barbecue. And kids love it too! If you're using wooden skewers, remember to soak them in water for about 20 minutes before threading them up so that they don't burn when you grill the skewers. Great served with rice or salad.

Serves 4

400g boneless, skinless chicken thighs, cut into cubes ....

3 leeks, cut into 3cm lengths

1 quantity Teriyaki & Ginger Sauce (*see* page 169), plus 1 tbsp sake (optional)

salt and black pepper

shichimi pepper or chilli flakes, to serve (optional)

Variation: Asparagus, cherry tomatoes or other green vegetables can be used instead of chicken.

1   Heat the grill to its highest setting.

2   Meanwhile, thread the chicken pieces and leek pieces alternately onto 4 skewers. Sprinkle over a little salt and pepper and grill for 5–7 minutes on each side.

3   Transfer the chicken skewers to a plate or serving dish and pour or brush the sauce over them. (The sake adds a lovely flavour, but you can leave it out if you don't want the extra calories or are serving the dish to children.)

4   Sprinkle with shichimi pepper or chilli flakes, if using, and serve immediately.

- 257 calories
- 8.2g saturated fat

Thai green curry with chicken & green beans

A super-easy, skinny and healthy supper. Serve with white or brown rice (*see* pages 44 and 45) for a more substantial meal.

Serves 4

1 tbsp light oil, such as groundnut, for frying

400g boneless, skinless chicken thighs, cut into bite-sized pieces

2 tbsp Thai green curry paste

2 shallots, finely sliced

1 tsp soy sauce

1 tsp fish sauce

200ml coconut milk

200g green beans, topped

2 tbsp mixed chopped coriander and basil, to serve

Variation: Use asparagus, broccoli or mangetout instead of green beans.

1   Place the oil in a pan over a high heat. When hot, briefly fry the chicken pieces until they start to brown.

2   Add the curry paste and stir to coat the chicken. Fry for another minute or so, then add the shallots, soy sauce and fish sauce.

3   Pour in the coconut milk and stir well. Bring to the boil, then simmer for 10 minutes.

4   Add the green beans, and a splash of water if the sauce is looking a bit reduced. Cover and cook for another 5 minutes, until the beans soften.

5   Spoon into a serving dish and sprinkle over the herbs to serve.

Grilled chicken teriyaki

In this recipe, you can also use breast meat instead of thighs, but make sure you reduce the cooking time slightly. It's delicious served on a bed of *Momofuku*-inspired rice plus some Pickled Cucumber with Ginger on the side (*see* pages 42 and 93).

Serves 2

1 tbsp light oil, such as groundnut, for frying

200g boneless, skinless chicken thighs

1 quantity Teriyaki & Ginger Sauce (*see* page 169)

1 tbsp sesame seeds, preferably toasted, to serve

1   Heat the grill to its highest setting.

2   Rub a little oil into the chicken and grill for about 5 minutes on each side.

3   Slice the chicken into large pieces and pour the sauce over them. Sprinkle with sesame seeds to serve.

- 256 calories
- 1.8g saturated fat

Steak teriyaki salad in lettuce cups

There's no need for knives and forks when eating these – just roll the filled lettuce leaves into mini bundles and eat using your fingers. Serve these colourful bites as a starter, a filling snack or as canapés with drinks at a party.

Serves 2

2 tsp light oil, such as groundnut, for frying

100g fillet or rump steak, cut into bite-sized slivers

4 iceberg or little gem lettuce leaves

¼ cucumber, cut into small cubes

small handful of radishes, thinly sliced lengthways

½ red onion, thinly sliced

small handful of coriander, chopped

1 quantity Teriyaki & Ginger Sauce (*see* page 169)

salt and black pepper

Nutritional tip: Buy smaller amounts of more expensive beef cuts like fillet, which is low in saturated fat and is a good source of anaemia-protective iron.

1   Heat a frying pan until really hot. Add the oil, then stir-fry the steak pieces for just a few minutes so that they are still pink inside. Transfer to a plate and season well with salt and pepper.

2   Put the lettuce leaves on a serving plate and fill with the cucumber, radishes, onion and coriander. Season with salt and pepper. Add the steak pieces, pour the sauce over them and serve.

- 148 calories
- 1.4g saturated fat

Seared beef with celeriac salad

Celeriac, as the name suggests, tastes like celery, but couldn't look more different. It's a knobbly vegetable that is best peeled with a small, sharp knife. Here it's used in a spicy, crunchy salad to accompany thinly sliced rare beef, and makes an elegant starter.

Serves 2

100g beef fillet, rump or sirloin

½ tsp light oil, such as groundnut, for frying

salt and black pepper

CELERIAC SALAD

2 tbsp soft/silken tofu

2 tbsp miso

1½ tsp wasabi paste

1 tsp lemon juice

½ head of celeriac, grated

1 tbsp mixed chopped chives and parsley

1   Season the beef well on both sides with salt and pepper.

2   Heat a frying pan until really hot. Add the oil, then fry the beef for 2 minutes on each side to get a lovely brown crust. Transfer to a plate to cool.

3   Blend or mix the tofu with the miso, wasabi and lemon juice to make a smooth paste. Put the celeriac into a bowl with the chives and parsley, then stir in the tofu mixture. Season with black pepper.

4   Slice the beef thinly and arrange on plates with the celeriac salad.

Nutritional tip: Wasabi is anti-bacterial, detoxifying and rich in vitamin C. It also aids digestion and is believed to stimulate the appetite.

- 263 calories
- 2.6g saturated fat

Seared miso-marinated steak

Marinating steak in miso gives it a deep umami flavour. Serve with some Easy Japanese-style Rice (*see* page 44) and Pickled Cucumber with Ginger (*see* page 93) for a healthy meal.

Serves 2

2 steaks (rump, sirloin or skirt), about 150g each

MARINADE

2 tbsp miso

1 tbsp sake

1 tbsp mirin

2 tsp sugar or sugar alternative

1 tbsp wasabi paste

1   To make the marinade, mix the miso with the sake in a large bowl to make a smooth paste. Stir in the other ingredients and mix well.

2   Put the steaks in the marinade and turn them over a few times to coat completely. Cover and refrigerate for up to 24 hours, but at least 15 minutes.

3   Heat a large frying pan until really hot. Add the oil, then fry the steaks for about 2 minutes on each side – depending on size and how well done you like them.

4   Transfer the steaks to a plate, then pour the remaining marinade into the empty pan. Heat for a few seconds so it reduces to a sauce.

5   Slice the steaks thickly, pour the sauce over them and serve.

FISH }

- 235 calories (with Herb Dressing), 275 calories (with Asian Pesto)
- 2.4g saturated fat (with Herb Dressing), 3.2g (with Asian Pesto)

Salmon & tuna tartar

Chopped raw fish with fiery wasabi and a herb dressing is an easy, colourful recipe to serve as an impressive starter. It's worth using a good fishmonger to buy the freshest possible fish you can find.

Serves 2

1 tsp sesame seeds, preferably toasted

1 tsp wasabi paste

1 tsp lime juice

1 tsp sesame oil

150g mixture of skinned salmon and tuna fillet, cut into small pieces

1 quantity Herb Dressing or Asian Pesto (see page 166)

baby cress or other small leaves, to serve

1   Put the sesame seeds, wasabi, lime juice and oil in a bowl and mix together. Add the fish and carefully fold into the sauce until completely coated.

2   Put a large spoonful of the fish on each plate and pour the dressing or pesto around it. Scatter with the baby cress or other small leaves to serve.

- 153 calories
- 1.7g saturated fat

Seared salmon & new-style sauce

Modern sushi chefs sear the outside of fish for added depth of flavour. They use a blowtorch, but it's also easy to do this in a really hot nonstick pan. You can serve this dish as sliced sashimi for a starter, or keep the salmon pieces whole and serve two as a main course with itsu's Special Salad (*see* page 84).

Serves 4 as a small plate

1 tsp light oil, such as groundnut, for frying

200g skinned salmon fillet ....

1 quantity New-style Sauce (*see* page 167)

Tip: Before searing fish, dry it well with kitchen paper – this helps to prevent it from sticking to the pan.

TO SERVE

2 chives, cut into 10cm lengths

1 slice of fresh root ginger, 10cm long, cut into fine strips

sesame seeds, preferably toasted

1   Heat a nonstick frying pan until really hot. Add the oil, then sear the salmon for about 1 minute on each side, until the outside is golden brown but the centre remains pink. Transfer to a plate to cool.

2   When ready to serve, cut the salmon into thin slices and arrange on serving plates.

3   Pour the sauce over the fish, garnish with the chives and ginger, then sprinkle with sesame seeds.

- 296 calories
- 2.8g saturated fat

Pan-fried salmon & wasabi peas

Thanks to Nicola Formby for this one. Nicola worked tirelessly with itsu over the years to help develop recipes and delicious sauces, and this dish is consistently one of her bestsellers. Bravo! At itsu we serve it as sashimi (*see* page 13), but it is also great as a main course.

Serves 2

1 tsp light oil, such as groundnut, for frying

2 skinned salmon fillets, about 100g each

½ quantity New-style Sauce (*see* page 167)

pea shoots, to garnish (optional)

PEAS

150g fresh or frozen petit pois

2 tbsp Spicy Sauce (*see* page 171)

1 tsp wasabi paste

large pinch of salt

½ tsp black pepper

1 First cook the peas in boiling, salted water for 2 minutes, then drain. Transfer them to a bowl and mix in the spicy sauce, wasabi, salt and pepper. Mash or blend the mixture for just a few seconds to lightly crush the peas. Set aside.

2 Heat a nonstick frying pan until really hot. Add the oil, then sear the salmon for about 1 minute on each side, until the outside is golden brown but the centre remains pink. Transfer to a plate to cool.

3 To serve, spoon the peas onto plates and place the salmon fillets on top. Pour a little of the new-style sauce over each serving and offer the rest separately. Garnish with pea shoots, if you like.

Nutritional tip: Peas are a great source of iron and fibre, including soluble fibre, which is good for regulating cholesterol.

Variation: Edamame (soya) beans or broad beans can be used instead of peas. Cook them in exactly the same way.

》》
- 270 calories
- 2.1g saturated fat

Salmon teriyaki We like to cook our salmon

so that it's served a little rare inside, which means it's juicier. Serve this yummy salmon on a bed of Japanese-style Rice with Spring Onion & Ginger Sauce or with itsu's Special Salad (*see* pages 42 or 84) with the sticky sauce drizzled over.

Serves 2

1 quantity Teriyaki & Ginger Sauce (*see* page 169)

1 tsp light oil, such as groundnut, for frying

2 skinned salmon fillets, about 100g each ....

{ **Nutritional tip:** Salmon is a great source of omega-3, and if you buy wild salmon, it contains less fat than the farmed variety.

1   Gently warm the sauce in a small saucepan.

2   Heat a nonstick frying pan until really hot, add the oil, then fry the salmon fillets for 2–4 minutes on each side, depending on their thickness, until the outside is brown and crisp while the inside remains a little pink.

3   Serve the salmon on a bed of rice or salad with the sauce poured over the top.

- 275 calories
- 2.8g saturated fat

Seared tuna with sesame & spicy sauce

Tuna and sesame seeds are made for each other. This super-healthy, easy main course is made extra-special with itsu's spicy sauce. It's great with a peppery leaf salad, such as rocket or mizuna, dressed with a drizzle of plain sesame oil or Yuzu-style Dressing (*see* page 170).

Serves 2

2 tuna steaks, about 130g each

1 tbsp soy sauce

1 tsp light oil, such as groundnut, for frying

TO SERVE

1 tbsp sesame seeds, preferably toasted

1 tsp chopped chives

peppery leaf salad

2–3 tbsp Spicy Sauce (*see* page 171)

Nutritional tips: Tuna is packed with omega 3s for a healthy heart and brain, while sesame seeds contain lots of magnesium, a mineral that is important for energy levels and a healthy nervous system. The seeds are also great for topping up levels of calcium, iron, zinc and essential fats.

1 Put the tuna steaks on a plate and pour the soy sauce over them. Turn to cover them completely in the sauce.

2 Heat a frying pan until really hot. Add the oil, then fry the tuna steaks for about 1 minute on each side so that the middle remains a little pink.

3 Serve each steak sprinkled with the sesame seeds and chives, and accompanied by peppery salad leaves, with the sauce offered alongside.

»
- 123 calories
- 1g saturated fat

Hot prawns with no-mayo mayonnaise

A beautiful pile of pink prawns on a bed of green spinach and rocket leaves: this is a lovely light meal, and great as a sharing plate too – just put it in the middle of the table for everyone to dip into.

Serves 2

100g uncooked peeled prawns, tails left on

1 tbsp light oil, such as groundnut, for frying

large pinch of salt

2 handfuls of mixed baby spinach and rocket leaves

1 quantity Sweet Citrus No-mayo Mayonnaise (*see* page 172)

chopped chives, to garnish

1 Rinse the prawns and dry well using a piece of kitchen paper.

2 Heat a frying pan or wok until really hot, then add the oil. Add the prawns and stir-fry for 2–3 minutes, until they start to colour, then sprinkle with the salt.

3 To serve, place a pile of leaves on each plate and arrange the prawns alongside, sprinkled with the chives. Serve with a bowl of the 'mayo' on the side, for dipping.

Variation: For a vegetarian alternative, use fried tofu instead of prawns.

Nutritional tip: Spinach is a great source of lutine, which protects the health of your eyes.

- 279 calories
- 2.1g saturated fat

Spicy prawn cocktail
Fresh, spicy prawns piled on a healthy, crunchy salad – this is seriously yummy yet light and full of goodness.

Serves 2 as a main course

150g cooked peeled prawns, tails discarded

2 tbsp Spicy Sauce (*see* page 171)

2 handfuls of mixed salad leaves

2 tsp sesame oil

CELERIAC SALAD

2 tbsp soft/silken tofu

2 tbsp miso

1½ tsp wasabi paste

½ head of celeriac, grated

1 tbsp mixed chopped chives and parsley

1   Put the prawns into a bowl and stir in the spicy sauce. Set aside.

2   Blend or mix the tofu with the miso and wasabi to make a smooth paste. Put the celeriac in a bowl with the chives and parsley and stir in the tofu mixture.

3   To serve, dress the salad leaves with the sesame oil and place some on each plate. Add a spoonful of the celeriac salad and place the spicy prawns on top.

Variation: Use Sweet Citrus No-mayo Mayonnaise (*see* page 172) instead of the Spicy Sauce.

FISH

143

- 99 calories
- 2.4g saturated fat

Tiger prawns with crisp garlic & chilli

You can serve these spicy titbits straight from the pan, dipping them in a Japanese-style no-mayo lemon, lime and orange sauce and eating them with your fingers. Alternatively, make them part of a simple summer lunch.

Serves 2

1 tsp light oil, such as groundnut, for frying

400g uncooked tiger prawns in their shells, tails left on (about 2 per person)

1 garlic clove, finely sliced

1 hot red Thai chilli, finely chopped

splash of soy sauce

1 quantity Sweet Citrus No-mayo Mayonnaise (*see* page 172)

lemon wedges, to serve

1   Heat a frying pan or wok until really hot, then add the oil. Add the prawns and fry for at least 1 minute on each side, until crisp and slightly brown. Transfer to a plate.

2   Add the garlic and chilli to the pan and fry for a few seconds, until starting to brown. Return the prawns to the pan, add a splash of soy sauce and toss together.

3   Serve with a bowl of sweet citrus mayonnaise and wedges of lemon on the side.

- 274 calories (plus 17 calories with the dipping sauce)
- 0.9g saturated fat (no extra fat with the dipping sauce)

Tiger prawn tempura
Fat, juicy tiger prawns in the lightest possible batter are delicious, especially if dipped in a zesty sauce. They are super-quick to make and also great to serve as finger food at parties. Note that the cooking oil can be reused; just cool and strain it, then store it in an airtight container.

Serves 2

200g uncooked peeled tiger prawns with tails left on

about 800ml sunflower oil, for deep-frying

1 quantity Ponzu Sauce (*see* page 169)

BATTER

100g plain flour

25g cornflour

1 tsp baking powder

½ tsp salt

200–250ml chilled sparkling water

Variation: For something really special, try these prawns as a filling in hand rolls (*see* page 62). Just don't forget to remove their tails first!

1   Sift the flours and baking powder into a bowl, then stir in the salt. Whisk in the water to make a smooth batter that has the consistency of pouring cream. Add more water if necessary.

2   Put the raw prawns on a plate next to the bowl of batter. Place a piece of kitchen paper on another plate.

3   In a deep saucepan or wok, heat the oil to 180°C or until a teaspoon of batter sizzles and starts to brown immediately.

4   Dip the prawns into the batter, then carefully lower them one at a time into the hot oil. Fry for about 1 minute, until the batter is puffy and golden then, using tongs, transfer them to the prepared plate. Fry the rest of the prawns in the same way.

5   Serve hot, offering the ponzu sauce in a bowl for dipping.

Spicy squid salad

Delicious served hot or cold, this salad is great for an easy starter and can be made in advance.

Serves 4

2 tsp light oil, such as groundnut, for frying

2 shallots, sliced

2 lime leaves, finely chopped

1 lemon grass stalk, finely chopped

1 hot red Thai chilli, finely chopped

200g baby squid with tentacles, cleaned ....

juice of 1 lime

2 tbsp mixed chopped coriander, basil and mint

100g bean sprouts

2 handfuls of mixed salad leaves

1 tbsp sesame oil

1 quantity Sweet Chilli Sauce (see page 167)

Nutritional tip: Just one serving of squid provides your daily requirement of the important antioxidant selenium.

1   Heat a frying pan, add the oil, then throw in the shallots, lime leaves, lemon grass and chilli. Fry for 2 minutes, until the shallots start to soften and colour slightly.

2   Add the squid and stir-fry on a high heat for just a minute or so, until the flesh turns white – any longer and it will become tough.

3   Pour over the lime juice and toss once more before removing from the heat.

4   Put the herbs, bean sprouts and salad leaves into a bowl, drizzle over the sesame oil and toss to coat.

5   To serve, put a small pile of the salad mixture on each plate, arrange the squid on top or alongside and pour a spoonful of sweet chilli sauce over each serving.

- 247 calories
- 2.3g saturated fat

Crispy chilli squid

At itsu we use karaage flour (potato starch) to give our squid a really crisp coating, but plain flour mixed half-and-half with cornflour is a great substitute. Try adding shichimi pepper to the flour if you like your food to have a fiery kick.

Serves 2

50g plain flour

50g cornflour

large pinch of salt

1 tsp shichimi pepper (optional)

200g baby squid with tentacles, cleaned and sliced into rings

about 600ml sunflower oil, for deep-frying

TO SERVE

1 red chilli, sliced

1 quantity Sweet Chilli Sauce (*see* page 167)

1 Combine the flours in a bowl and add the salt and shichimi pepper (if using). Toss the squid in the flour.

2 In a deep pan or wok, heat the oil to 180°C, or until a piece of floured squid sizzles and starts to brown immediately.

3 Carefully add a handful of squid at a time to the hot oil. Fry for just 1 minute – any longer and it will become tough – then drain on kitchen paper while you cook the next batch.

4 To serve, sprinkle the chilli over the squid and offer the sauce in a small bowl for dipping.

Scallop salad with chilli, spring onions & crisp garlic

Ideal for a quick supper or an elegant starter, these scallops can be served hot or cold, so it's a great dish to prepare ahead of time.

Serves 2

2 tsp light oil, such as groundnut, for frying

1 garlic clove, finely sliced

100g scallops (2 large or 3 medium per person)

1 hot red Thai chilli, finely sliced

1 large spring onion, sliced

1 tbsp soy sauce

2 handfuls of rocket or mixed peppery salad leaves

2 handfuls of bean sprouts

1 tbsp Yuzu-style Dressing (*see* page 170)

Nutritional tip: Scallops are a source of zinc, which helps maintain a healthy immune system.

1   Heat a frying pan or wok until really hot. Add the oil, then stir-fry the garlic for a few seconds, until golden. Transfer to a plate, making sure you get all the bits out so there are none left to burn.

2   Add the scallops to the pan and fry for just 1–2 minutes on each side.

3   Add the chilli and spring onion and cook for another minute to soften slightly. Pour over the soy sauce, give it a quick stir and remove from the heat.

4   Mix the leaves and bean sprouts in a bowl with the dressing. Toss well and divide between 2 plates. Place 2 or 3 scallops alongside each pile of leaves, add some of the spring onion and chilli, and sprinkle the crisp garlic over the top.

Mackerel with sweet mirin sauce

Fresh mackerel is unbelievably good for you because it contains the highest amount of omega-3 fatty acids in any fish. The sweet sauce used here makes the ideal accompaniment to its rich, oily flavour. This is great served with rice and Pickled Cucumber with Ginger (*see* page 93).

Serves 2

2 tsp sake

2 tsp mirin

1 tbsp soy sauce

10g or 2cm fresh root ginger, grated

1 tsp light oil, such as groundnut, for frying

2 fresh mackerel fillets, skin on

1   Mix the sake, mirin, soy sauce and ginger in a small bowl. Set aside.

2   Heat a nonstick frying pan, add the oil, and cook the mackerel for about 2 minutes on each side, until the skin is crisp and the flesh is lightly browned. Pour the sauce into the pan and turn off the heat. It will sizzle and reduce slightly and coat the fish.

3   Cut each fillet in half. Serve on a bed of rice with pickled cucumber with ginger, if you like.

- 110 calories
- 0.4g saturated fat

Baked sea bass with ginger & spring onion

Steaming the fish in little foil pouches makes this an easy, mess-free meal. The other ingredients all infuse into the fish to give it a fragrant, delicious flavour. Serve with Spinach Balls with Sesame Sauce (*see* page 94) for the perfect easy dinner.

Serves 2

2 skinned sea bass fillets, about
100g each

2 spring onions, sliced

10g or 2cm fresh root ginger, sliced

2 tbsp soy sauce

black pepper

steamed pak choi or other vegetables,
to serve

1   Preheat the oven to 200°C/fan 180°C/gas mark 6.

2   Cut two A4-sized sheets of foil and lay a sea bass fillet on each one. Scatter over the spring onions, ginger and pepper, then fold up the foil, scrunching the edges together, but leaving a small gap in the top of each parcel. Pour the soy sauce into the gap, then seal the parcels completely.

3   Bake for 8–10 minutes, then carefully unwrap the parcels and transfer the fish to plates, pouring the sauce over the top. Serve with your chosen vegetables.

- 90 calories (with Sweet Chilli Sauce), 109 calories (with Herb Dressing), 129 calories (with Asian Pesto)
- 0.3g saturated fat (with Sweet Chilli Sauce), 0.6g (with Herb Dressing), 1g (with Asian Pesto)

Crab crystal rolls
Once you realize how surprisingly easy these rolls are to make, you can play around with the ingredients, perhaps adding green beans instead of asparagus, or trying different leaves and herbs.

Serves 4

100g cooked crabmeat

2 tsp lemon juice

10g thin glass noodles

4 asparagus spears

4 outer leaves of little gem lettuce

1 tsp chopped chives

2 tbsp coriander leaves

4 spring roll wrappers

salt and black pepper

dipping sauce, such as Sweet Chilli Sauce, Herb Dressing or Asian Pesto (*see* pages 166–7)

1   Put the crabmeat into a bowl, add the lemon juice and some black pepper. Stir to combine, then set aside.

2   Put the noodles into a large heatproof bowl and cover them with boiling water. Leave for 3 minutes (or as per the packet instructions), then drain and refresh under cold water.

3   Cook the asparagus in boiling, salted water for 3 minutes, then drain and refresh. Cut in half lengthways.

4   Cut the stalks out of the lettuce leaves and tear them in half.

5   Place all the prepared ingredients, together with the herbs, around a clean board. Fill a large bowl with boiling water.

6   Dampen the board slightly where you will prepare the rolls, then dip a wrapper into the boiling water, turning it until wet all over. Don't allow it to stay too long in the water – when finished, it should still feel a little firm. Lay the sheet flat on the damp board, trying to avoid creasing it.

7   Arrange a tablespoon of crabmeat in a strip on the wrapper, just above the centre, leaving a 2.5cm gap at each end. Sprinkle over one-quarter of the herbs, then place 2 halved lettuce leaves on top. Add a layer of cooked noodles, and finally 2 slices of asparagus.

8   Lift the top edge of the wrapper, bring it down over the layered filling and tuck it underneath. Now roll it towards you, folding in the sides as you go so that they are sealed inside the roll. The sheet will stick to itself, leaving you with one long roll, sealed at both ends. Cut it in half diagonallly and set aside while you make the other rolls.

9   Arrange the halved rolls on a serving platter with a bowl of the dipping sauce in the middle, or serve 2 halves per person, offering the sauce separately.

- 66 calories
- 1g saturated fat

Prawn crystal rolls At itsu we make these rolls twice a day, not only because they are quick and easy, but so that they also taste their freshest. These thin spring roll wrappers (available from most big supermarkets and Asian food shops) have a beautiful translucent quality when wet.

Serves 4

4 spring roll wrappers

½ avocado, stoned and thinly sliced

1 carrot, shaved into strips using a potato peeler

¼ cucumber, deseeded and cut into strips

a few lettuce leaves (little gem, cos or iceberg), firm stalks removed

50g cooked peeled prawns, tails discarded

4 tsp Asian Pesto or Herb Dressing (see page 166)

4 pinches of shichimi pepper or chilli flakes

1 quantity Sweet Chilli Sauce (see page 167), or any other favourite dipping sauce, to serve

1   Place all the ingredients around a clean board. Fill a large bowl with boiling water.

2   Dampen the board slightly where you will prepare the rolls, then dip a wrapper into the boiling water, turning it until wet all over. Don't allow it to stay too long in the water – when finished, it should still feel a little firm. Lay the sheet flat on the damp board, trying to avoid creasing it.

3   Lay a few slices of avocado along the wrapper, just above the centre, leaving a 2.5cm gap at each end. Add a few strips of the carrot and cucumber, then a few torn strips of lettuce.

4   Take about 1 tablespoon of the prawns and sprinkle them along the lettuce. Pour a teaspoon of the Asian pesto or herb dressing over them and add a good pinch of shichimi pepper or chilli flakes.

5   Lift the top edge of the wrapper over the layered filling and tuck it underneath. Now roll it towards you, folding in the sides as you go so that they are sealed inside the roll. The sheet will stick to itself, leaving you with one long roll, sealed at both ends. Cut it in half diagonallly and set aside while you make the other rolls.

6   Serve 2 halves per person, offering the sweet chilli sauce separately for dipping.

- 87 calories
- 1.1g saturated fat

Spicy tuna crystal rolls Fresh tuna is absolutely

delicious in these rolls, but very fresh salmon fillet or our cooked tangy tuna mix (*see* page 79) are great alternatives. Choose your favourite dipping sauce, to serve.

Serves 4

100g very fresh tuna, chopped

4 tbsp Spicy Sauce (*see* page 171)

4 outer leaves of little gem, cos or iceberg lettuce, firm stalks removed

½ carrot, shaved into strips using a potato peeler

¼ avocado, stoned and thinly sliced

1 tsp chopped chives

4 spring roll wrappers

1 quantity Sweet Chilli Sauce (*see* page 167), or any other favourite dipping sauce, to serve

1   Put the chopped tuna into a bowl and mix in the spicy sauce.

2   Place all the remaining ingredients around a clean board. Fill a large bowl with boiling water.

3   Dampen the board slightly where you will prepare the rolls, then dip a wrapper into the boiling water, turning it until wet all over. Don't allow it to stay too long in the water – when finished, it should still feel a little firm. Lay the sheet flat on the damp board, trying to avoid creasing it.

4   Lay a quarter of the tuna in a long strip on the wrapper, just above the centre, leaving a 2.5cm gap at each end. Tear a lettuce leaf in half and place over the tuna. Add some carrot and avocado strips as the next layer, then sprinkle with the chives.

5   Lift the top edge of the wrapper over the layered filling and tuck it underneath. Now roll it towards you, folding in the sides as you go so that they are sealed inside the roll. The sheet will stick to itself, leaving you with one long roll, sealed at both ends. Cut it in half diagonallly and set aside while you make the other rolls.

6   Serve 2 halves per person, offering your choice of sauce separately for dipping.

DRESSINGS & SAUCES

- 6 calories
- trace saturated fat

Homemade dashi stock

Dashi, a simple stock, is a very important ingredient in Japanese cooking because it forms the flavour base for most soups. Unlike French stocks, which take hours to make, dashi is quick and easy to put together because you need only two ingredients plus water. Kombu and bonito flakes are readily available from Japanese suppliers (*see* page 188). Stored in an airtight container, the dashi will keep for up to three days in the fridge, or it can be frozen.

Serves 2 (makes about 800ml)

2 large pieces of kombu

1 litre water

30g bonito flakes

1   Wipe the kombu with a damp cloth, then place in a pan with the water and leave to soften for about 30 minutes.

2   When the kombu is soft, place the pan over the heat and bring almost to the boil. Take off the heat and discard the kombu.

3   Add the bonito flakes to the hot water and leave to steep (off the heat) for 10 minutes.

4   Strain the liquid into a clean container, discarding the bonito flakes.

5   Use the stock immediately, or store as recommended above until needed.

- 63 calories
- 0.8g saturated fat

- 43 calories
- 0.4g saturated fat

Asian pesto

Here's a herby, fresh dressing to add some zing to your salads or crystal rolls. You can also use it in recipes as an alternative to Herb Dressing (*see* right). Stored in a screwtop jar, it will keep for up to a week in the fridge.

Serves 4

large bunch of coriander

a few sprigs of mint

2 spring onions

1 hot red Thai chilli, deseeded

1 tbsp ready-made pickled ginger or grated fresh root ginger

1 garlic clove, grated or crushed

2 tbsp sesame oil

1 tbsp soy sauce

1 tbsp lemon juice

1 tsp sugar or sugar alternative

½ tsp salt

1   Put all the ingredients into a blender and whizz to a smooth sauce with flecks of herbs. Alternatively, hand-chop the herbs, onions, chilli and ginger as finely as possible. Place in a bowl, add the remaining ingredients and mix well.

2   Use the sauce immediately, or store in a screwtop jar in the fridge until needed.

Herb dressing

This vibrantly green and creamy dressing can be used on all sorts of dishes, such as Salmon & Tuna Tartar (*see* page 131). It's also great as a salad dressing or a dipping sauce. Stored in a screwtop jar, it will keep for up to a week in the fridge.

Serves 4

large bunch of coriander

1 tbsp soft/silken tofu

2 lime leaves

1 tsp grated fresh root ginger

1 tbsp brown sugar or sugar alternative

1 tsp rice vinegar

1 tsp fish sauce

1 tsp lime juice

1 tbsp sesame oil

1   To achieve the best consistency, put all the ingredients into a blender and whizz to make a smooth sauce.

2   Use immediately, or store in a screwtop jar in the fridge until needed.

- 48 calories
- 0.2g saturated fat

- 77 calories
- 0.8g saturated fat

Sweet chilli sauce

This fresh and punchy dipping sauce goes with lots of dishes, such as crystal rolls, chillied squid and mini pork burgers. It can also be used as a dressing for spicy salads. Stored in a screwtop jar, the sauce will keep for up to two weeks in the fridge.

Serves 2

2 tbsp fish sauce

1 tbsp palm sugar, brown sugar or sugar alternative

1 tbsp rice vinegar

1 tsp lime juice

1 tsp lemon juice

½ tsp grated fresh root ginger

½ hot red Thai chilli, finely chopped

1 tsp sesame oil

1   Put the fish sauce into a bowl, add the sugar and stir until dissolved. Add the remaining ingredients and stir again.

2   Use the sauce immediately, or store in a screwtop jar in the fridge until needed.

New-style sauce

Salty and zingy all at once, this is a great dressing for sesame-coated grilled salmon or pan-fried mackerel. Stored in a screwtop jar, it will keep for up to two weeks in the fridge.

Serves 2

1 garlic clove, grated or crushed

4 tbsp soy sauce

10g or 2cm fresh root ginger, grated

1 tsp lemon juice

2 tsp mirin

1 tbsp sesame oil

1   Put all the ingredients into a bowl and stir well.

2   Use the sauce immediately, or store in a screwtop jar in the fridge until needed.

- 43 calories
- 0g saturated fat

Miso dressing

A great dressing to use on salads, vegetables and even rice. We use sweet miso, which is paler and less salty than other types, but try experimenting with red (dark) miso too. Stored in a screwtop jar, it will keep for up to two weeks in the fridge.

Serves 2

2 tbsp miso paste

1 tbsp mirin

2 tsp rice vinegar

1 tsp lemon juice

1 tbsp water

black pepper

1 Put the miso into a bowl, add the mirin and mix to make a smooth paste. Add the remaining ingredients and stir well.

2 Use the dressing immediately, or store in a screwtop jar in the fridge until needed.

- 121 calories
- 1.3g saturated fat

Sesame sauce

A favourite at itsu, this creamy, nutty sauce is served with tenderstem broccoli or steamed spinach, but could also be used as a dressing for soba noodles, as a dip for crudités, or spooned over grilled tuna or chicken. Stored in a screwtop jar, the sauce will keep for up to two weeks in the fridge.

Serves 4

4 tbsp mirin

3 tbsp tahini paste

1 tbsp soy sauce

3 tbsp lemon juice

1 tsp sesame oil

1 tsp sugar or sugar alternative

1 small garlic clove, grated or crushed

1 tbsp water

1 Put all the ingredients into a bowl and stir well to make a smooth sauce.

2 Use the sauce immediately, or store in a screwtop jar in the fridge until needed.

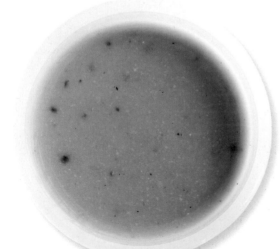

- 86 calories
- 0g saturated fat

- 17 calories
- 0g saturated fat

Teriyaki & ginger sauce

This super-tasty sauce can be used in many different ways – on grilled chicken, salmon or steak; poured over rice; or to dress salads. Sweet yet salty, it is full of goodness. Stored in a screwtop jar, it will keep for up to two weeks in the fridge. If the sauce thickens slightly during storage, loosen it with a little water before use.

Serves 2

3 tbsp mirin

3 tbsp soy sauce

1 tbsp sugar or sugar alternative

2 tsp rice vinegar

1 tsp cornflour

20g or 4cm fresh root ginger, grated

1 Put all the ingredients into a small saucepan and stir well. Bring to the boil and bubble for a couple of minutes, stirring constantly, to reduce and form a thick syrup.

2 Use the sauce immediately, or store in a screwtop jar in the fridge until needed.

Ponzu sauce

This is a great citrussy, salty sauce for dipping tempura or sashimi. Stored in a screwtop jar, it will keep for up to two weeks in the fridge.

Serves 2

4 tbsp soy sauce

4 tsp mirin

3 tsp orange or mandarin juice

1 tsp lemon or lime juice

1 Put all the ingredients into a blender and whizz to make a smooth sauce.

2 Use the sauce immediately, or store in a screwtop jar in the fridge until needed.

Variation: If you can find bottled yuzu juice, use 4 teaspoons of it instead of the other fruit juices.

Nutritional tip: Ginger contains anti-inflammatory components, and some people swear it helps ease their joints. It's also a good tummy soother.

Miso hollandaise

Despite containing no butter or eggs – major constituents of traditional hollandaise – this version has all the creamy richness you'd hope for. Serve with grilled asparagus, or on new potatoes or other lightly steamed seasonal vegetables. Stored in a screwtop jar, it will keep for up to two weeks in the fridge.

Serves 2 with a main course

4 tbsp soft/silken tofu

2 tsp soy sauce

4 tbsp miso paste

2 tsp rice vinegar

3 tsp lemon juice

black pepper

1   Put all the ingredients into a bowl or blender and whizz to make a smooth sauce.

2   Use immediately, or store in a screwtop jar in the fridge until needed.

Yuzu-style dressing

Pimp up your salad leaves with this easy citrus-flavoured dressing. The Japanese fruit called 'yuzu' looks like a small, knobbly grapefruit and tastes tart but sweet. You can buy yuzu juice from specialist Japanese suppliers (*see* page 188), but the combination of juices listed below makes a yummy alternative. Stored in a screwtop jar, the dressing will keep for up to two weeks in the fridge.

Serves 4

1 tbsp soy sauce

1 tbsp mandarin or orange juice

1 tsp lime juice

1 tsp lemon juice

2 tbsp sesame oil or other light oil

black pepper

1   Put all the ingredients into a small bowl and whisk well.

2   Use immediately, or store in a screwtop jar in the fridge until needed.

Nutritional tip: Full of vitamin C from the citrus juices and made with no added salt, this dressing is a really healthy option.

- 64 calories
- 0.7g saturated fat

Spicy sauce At itsu

you'll find spicy sauce everywhere that mayo usually appears. It contains 74 per cent less fat than mayo and tastes ten times as good. Use this delicious sauce on seared salmon sashimi, as well as on smoked chicken, prawns and even in sushi. Stored in a screwtop jar, it will keep for up to two weeks in the fridge. If the sauce thickens slightly during storage, loosen it with a little lemon juice or water before use.

Serves 6

120g soft/silken tofu

3 tsp tahini paste

3 tsp Sriracha chilli sauce or 1 hot red Thai chilli, chopped

2 tbsp lemon juice

3 tsp sugar or sugar alternative

10g or 2cm fresh root ginger, grated

2 garlic cloves, grated or crushed

1½ tsp black pepper

½ tsp salt

1 tbsp water

1 tbsp light oil, such as groundnut or grapeseed

1   Put all the ingredients into a blender and whizz to make a smooth sauce.

2   Use the sauce immediately, or store in a screwtop jar in the fridge until needed.

- 122 calories
- 0.9g saturated fat

Toasted pumpkin seed topping These seeds

make a great salty, crunchy topping for potsus or salads, and are also delicious as a healthy snack. Stored in a screwtop jar, they will keep for up to two weeks in a cupboard.

Serves 2

40g pumpkin seeds

2 tbsp soy sauce

1   Heat a dry frying pan. When hot, add the pumpkin seeds and toast for just 1 minute, tossing occasionally, until they start to crackle and brown.

2   Turn off the heat and pour over the soy sauce, which will bubble dramatically and then settle.

3   Scrape the mixture into a bowl and eat piping hot, or leave to cool, then store in a screwtop jar until needed.

Shallot dressing

Sweet, caramelized shallots with a peppery wasabi kick: this is a dangerously moreish and yummy dressing for salads, and also great served with grilled chicken or steak. Stored in a screwtop jar, it will keep for up to two weeks in the fridge.

Serves 4

1 tbsp light oil, such as groundnut, for frying

2–3 small shallots, minced (you can do this with a stick blender)

1 tbsp water

2 tsp sugar or sugar alternative

3 tbsp soy sauce

2 tbsp rice wine vinegar

10g or 2cm fresh root ginger, grated

1 tsp black pepper

½ tsp wasabi powder or 1 tsp wasabi paste

1 tbsp sesame oil

1 Heat the oil in a small saucepan. Add the shallots, water and sugar then cover and cook on a low heat for 10 minutes.

2 Meanwhile, mix all the remaining ingredients, except the sesame oil, in a bowl.

3 When the shallots are soft, sweet and a little brown, add them to the soy mixture. Pour in the sesame oil and stir well.

4 Use the sauce immediately, or store in a screwtop jar in the fridge until needed.

Sweet citrus no-mayo mayonnaise

At itsu we never use mayo. Once you've tried this alternative, you won't either! It's not only a delicious dip for crisp-fried prawns or tempura, but it also makes a great salad dressing. Stored in a screwtop jar, it will keep for up to two weeks in the fridge.

Serves 4

4 tbsp soft/silken tofu

1 tbsp sesame oil

1 tbsp mandarin or orange juice

1 tsp lemon juice

1 tsp lime juice

1 tsp soy sauce

½ tsp wasabi paste

1 small shallot, grated or finely chopped

1 tbsp ready-made pickled ginger, finely chopped

1 For the best texture, put all the ingredients into a blender and whizz until smooth.

2 Use the sauce immediately, or store in a screwtop jar in the fridge until needed.

- 56 calories
- 2.4g saturated fat

ithai sauce
After years of tweaking, we have created a unique and delicious Thai sauce with the perfect balance of infused flavours. It's something we are truly proud of, and its place as an itsu classic is now secure. Use it on potsus, as a dressing for steamed vegetables, or poured over white or brown rice. Stored in a screwtop jar, it will keep for up to a week in the fridge.

Serves 4

4 tbsp coconut milk

1 tsp tomato passata

4–6 lime leaves, finely chopped

½ lemon grass stalk, finely chopped

10g or 2cm fresh root ginger, grated

1 garlic clove, grated or crushed

1 shallot, finely chopped

2 tsp ground cumin

2 tsp lemon juice

1 tsp fish sauce

1 tsp soy sauce

1 tsp crushed chilli or ½ red hot Thai chilli, chopped

1 tsp sugar or sugar alternative

1 tsp tamarind paste

1 tsp cornflour

½ tsp salt

160ml water

1 tbsp coriander leaves, chopped

1 Put all the ingredients, except the water and coriander leaves, into a blender and whizz to a smooth sauce. Alternatively, hand-chop the ingredients as finely as possible and combine in a bowl.

2 Put the sauce into a small saucepan and add the water. Slowly bring to the boil, stirring, then reduce the heat to a simmer and cook for 5 minutes.

3 Use the sauce immediately, adding the coriander to serve, or store in a screwtop jar in the fridge until needed.

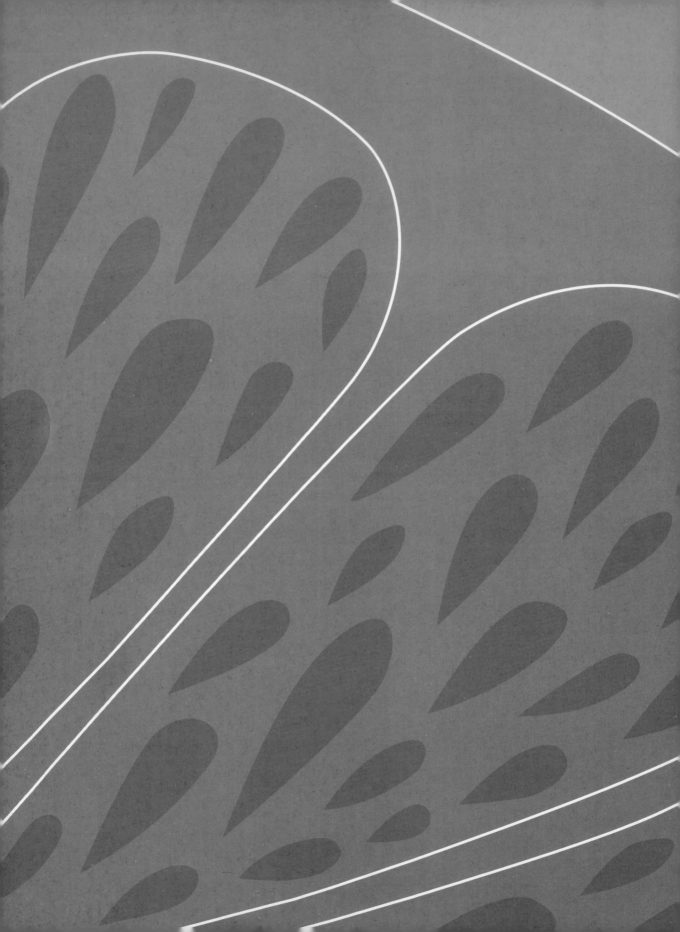

DESSERTS }
& DRINKS }

- 121 calories
- 0.1g saturated fat

Hawaii five-fruit

This is our favourite fruit salad mix. If covered, it will keep in the fridge for several hours; alternatively, put it in a plastic pot as a portable healthy snack or for a great picnic dessert.

Serves 4

½ medium mango, about 150g

½ medium melon, about 300g

½ pineapple, about 300g

150g blueberries

150g pomegranate seeds

zest and juice of ½ lemon

zest and juice of ½ lime

1 tbsp clear honey, or any sugar alternative

1 Peel the mango, melon and pineapple, and discard the melon seeds. Cut the flesh into bite-sized pieces and mix in a bowl with the blueberries and pomegranate seeds.

2 Combine the lemon and lime juice in a small bowl, then add the honey and stir until dissolved.

3 Pour the honey mixture over the fruit and stir to combine.

Nutritional tip: Brightly coloured fruits are loaded with antioxidants. Pomegranates and blueberries are said to help regulate blood pressure.

- 221 calories
- 5.4g saturated fat

White chocolate yogurt & fruits

A rich, yummy pudding, this tastes decadent but is still butterfly light. Covered in nutritious fruit, it's a proper healthy treat.

Serves 2

50g white chocolate, broken into small pieces, or white chocolate drops

250g low-fat natural yogurt

1 tsp vanilla extract

150g mixture of fresh blueberries, raspberries and blackberries, or whatever berries you fancy

1   Put the chocolate into a heatproof bowl and melt in the microwave for 1 minute on High. Alternatively, sit the bowl over a small saucepan of simmering water (it must not actually touch the water) and warm over a medium heat until melted.

2   Mix the yogurt with the vanilla extract and slowly add this mixture to the melted chocolate, mixing well to get a smooth consistency.

3   To serve, spoon the yogurt mixture into cups or bowls and sprinkle the berries on top.

»
- 278 calories
- 0.4g saturated fat

Baked bananas with no-dairy custard
Baking hot, sweet bananas coated in a creamy, caramel sauce made with dairy-free soft tofu. What could be more tempting?

Serves 2

2 very ripe bananas, unpeeled ....

zest and juice of ½ orange

1 tbsp brown sugar or sugar alternative

100g soft/silken tofu

50g sugar or sugar alternative

Nutritional tip: Bananas are full of potassium, vitamin B and magnesium – all essential for good health.

1   Preheat the oven to 220°C/fan 200°C/gas mark 7.

2   Slice the bananas in half lengthways and place them in a small baking dish. Sprinkle the orange zest, juice and brown sugar over them. Bake for 20 minutes.

3   Meanwhile, put the tofu into a bowl and whisk to a smooth paste.

4   Place the remaining sugar in a saucepan with 2 tablespoons water, bring to the boil and continue boiling until it starts to turn brown and caramelize. Pour into the tofu and whisk well to combine.

5   Serve the bananas hot, with the caramel tofu alongside for pouring over them.

- 232 calories
- 8.3g saturated fat

Classic chocolate mousse Find some
sweet little serving pots or cups for the perfect portion size – small is beautiful when it comes to rich puddings. A hint of ginger gives these mini treats a subtle kick.

Serves 4

100g good-quality dark chocolate, at least 70% cocoa solids, broken into small pieces

2 tsp mirin

1 tbsp golden syrup

6 free-range eggs

40g or 8cm fresh root ginger, grated

1   Put the chocolate, mirin and syrup into a heatproof bowl and melt in the microwave for 1 minute on High. Alternatively, sit the bowl over a small saucepan of simmering water (it must not actually touch the water) and warm over a medium heat until melted.

2   Meanwhile, separate the eggs, putting the whites into a clean, grease-free bowl and the yolks into another. Set aside.

3   Place a sieve over the bowl of egg yolks. Hold the grated ginger in your hand over the sieve and squeeze the juice from it (you should get about a teaspoonful). Stir the juice into the yolks along with a tablespoon of water.

4   When the chocolate has melted, pour it slowly into the yolk mixture, stirring constantly until smooth.

5   Whisk the egg whites until they form soft peaks – try not to overwhisk them, or the mousse will become too stiff. When they are ready, gently but thoroughly fold them into the chocolate mixture so they are completely combined.

6   Pour the mousse into small cups, ramekins or shallow serving dishes and place in the freezer for 20 minutes to chill or transfer to the fridge if not eating it straight away.

Nutritional tip: Good-quality dark chocolate contains anthocyanidins, which help regulate blood flow, and is also a good source of magnesium, which boosts energy levels.

»
- 168 calories
- 1.9g saturated fat

Mixed berry frozen yogurt
At itsu we use super-healthy pomegranate, blueberries and strawberries in our frozen yogurt because they're packed with all the vitamins you need for a healthy life. Why not make double quantities and freeze the rest to enjoy another day?

Serves 2

2 tbsp honey, or any sugar alternative

200g natural yogurt (any type you like)

200g mixed frozen berries

1 Chill 2 small bowls in the freezer.

2 Put the honey and yogurt into a blender and whizz together. Add the berries and whizz again.

3 Spoon the mixture into the chilled bowls and serve immediately.

Variation: Use any frozen fruit you like; just remember to freeze it in small pieces so that it blends easily.

Nutritional tip: As well as being a good source of vitamin C, berries are rich in anthocyanins, which help maintain firm skin and flexible arteries, and they're good for your memory too.

»
- 99 calories
- 1.7g saturated fat

Green tea iced smoothie
Whizz up this refreshing, energy-boosting smoothie in the morning for breakfast, or pop it into a flask and enjoy as a low-calorie snack to perk you up during the day. It uses matcha, a powder made from ground green tea leaves.

Serves 2

handful of ice cubes

200g natural yogurt (any type you like)

1 tbsp honey, or any sugar alternative

1 tsp matcha

1 Put all the ingredients into a blender and whizz together until creamy and smooth.

2 Pour into tall glasses and serve while it's still ice-cold.

Nutritional tip: Yogurt is full of bone-building calcium, while green tea is famed for its antioxidant properties, and is thought to protect against heart disease too.

Pomegranate, pineapple & mint salad with lime syrup

Pomegranate seeds not only look and taste delicious, but they contain many powerful antioxidants. Here they are paired with sweet pineapple and refreshing mint to make a simple yet delicious salad.

Serves 2

300g pineapple

seeds from ½ pomegranate (about 100g)

a few mint leaves

30g sugar or sugar alternative

2 tbsp water

juice and zest of 1 lime

1   Cut the skin off the pineapple and cut the flesh into small pieces. Transfer it to a small bowl and sprinkle with the pomegranate seeds and mint leaves.

2   Put the sugar and water into a small saucepan and bring to the boil. Continue boiling for 2 minutes to form a syrup. Remove from the heat and add the lime juice and zest.

3   Pour the hot syrup over the fruit and eat immediately, or cover and keep cool until required.

- 270 calories
- 2.1g saturated fat

Quick watermelon & lime sorbet

Here's a really easy sorbet. If you freeze the watermelon in the morning, you can make it that night and enjoy it as a skinny dessert treat.

Serves 4

½ small watermelon (about 700g)

3 tbsp sugar or sugar alternative

4 tbsp lime juice

1. Peel the watermelon and cut the flesh into small chunks (you can leave the seeds in). Place in a bowl and freeze overnight, or for at least 4 hours.

2. Put the frozen watermelon into a large blender, add the sugar and lime juice and whizz to a smooth sorbet. Serve immediately.

Nutritional tip: Watermelon contains the same antioxidants that are found in tomatoes. They contribute towards a healthy heart and are great to eat in the sun as they offer some natural UV protection.

»
- 56 calories
- no saturated fat

Detox zinger juice

You don't need a juicer to make this super-healthy juice, which contains a special blend of spices to help detox your body. It keeps for three days in the fridge.

Serves 4

150ml beetroot juice (available from most supermarkets)

400ml apple juice

juice of ½ lemon

pinch of ground cloves

¼ tsp ground cinnamon

¼ tsp ground turmeric

250ml water

Nutritional tip: Beetroot is believed to lower blood pressure and help repair muscles after exercise, while turmeric has anti-inflammatory properties.

1   Put all the ingredients in a lidded container and shake well.

2   Serve chilled, or bottle and carry with you as a portable health kick.

»
- 51 calories
- no saturated fat

Ginger & melon zinger

Whizz up this delicious mixture in a blender for a healthy breakfast juice. If you want to store some, it will keep, in a sealed container, for up to two days in the fridge.

Serves 4

300g melon pieces (any type)

300ml apple juice

10g or 2cm fresh root ginger, grated

juice of 1 lime

150ml water

1   Put all the ingredients into a blender and whizz until smooth. Chill until needed, or serve with ice cubes for an instant, refreshing drink.

Nutritional tip: Ginger is anti-inflammatory – a great stomach soother.

- 20 calories
- no saturated fat

Iced i-tea

A refreshing beverage for a hot summer's day, this drink is based on green tea and is great for boosting the metabolism.

Serves 4

4 green tea bags

20g or 4cm fresh root ginger, sliced

4–6 sprigs of mint

1 tbsp honey, or any sugar alternative

juice of 1 lemon

800ml boiling water

2 handfuls of ice cubes

TO SERVE
ice cubes
lemon slices
mint leaves

1 Put the tea bags, ginger, mint, honey and lemon juice into a large bowl, add the boiling water and steep for 5 minutes.

2 Remove just the tea bags, then add the ice cubes. Chill in the fridge or freezer until needed.

3 Before serving, strain the liquid into a clean jug and serve with ice cubes, lemon slices and mint leaves.

Left: Iced i-tea
Right: Ginger & melon zinger
Back: Detox zinger juice

Stockists

All the ingredients in the recipes in this book are easy to find. Many are available from major supermarkets, and more specialist ingredients can be found easily online or in good Japanese or Asian food stores. Some excellent online sources are listed below. Listed too are some Japanese and Asian food stockists that we recommend, and a few great fish shops stocking sashimi-grade fish as well as Japanese groceries.

GOOD ONLINE SOURCES

Amazon.co.uk – has a good variety of products sourced from different suppliers.

Clearspring.co.uk – manufactures an extensive range of good-quality Japanese ingredients.

Japancentre.com – Japanese food shop in Regent Street, London, which also has a good online service.

Japanesekitchen.co.uk – has an extensive range of good-value ingredients.

Mitoku.com – this Japanese food manufacturer's website does not sell to the public, but it offers useful information about Japanese food.

Mountfuji.co.uk – offers a wide range of Japanese ingredients.

Sainsburys.co.uk – the online arm of Sainsbury's has a good-value selection of Japanese ingredients, all of which can be found in-store too.

Souschef.co.uk – an easy-to-navigate, good-value site, with a broad range and well-packaged delivery.

Tazakifoods.co.uk – a good site for really specialist ingredients; has a wide range of Yutaka-brand products, which we recommend.

Tesco.com – the online arm of Tesco has a good-value selection of Japanese ingredients, all of which can be found in-store too.

Theasiancookshop.co.uk – has a wide variety of Japanese foodstuffs, but some products can be expensive.

TK Trading (japan-foods.co.uk) – offers a wide variety of Japanese ingredients and cooking utensils.

Waitrose.com – the online arm of Waitrose has a good range of Japanese ingredients at reasonable prices, all of which can be found in-store too.

OUR FAVOURITE FOOD SHOPS

Arigato
48–50 Brewer Street
London W1F 9TG

Atari-ya
For shop locations see atariya.co.uk

Japan Centre
19 Shaftesbury Avenue
London W1D 7ED

La Petite Poissonnerie
75a Gloucester Avenue
London NW1 8LD
lapetite-poissonnerie.co.uk

Moxon's Fishmongers
Various branches around London
moxonsfreshfish.com

Rex Goldsmith
The Chelsea Fishmonger
10 Cale Street
London SW3 3QU
thechelseafishmonger.co.uk

Kensington Place Fish shop
201 Kensington Church Street
London W8 7LX
kensingtonplace-restaurant.co.uk

Wholefoods
For shop locations see wholefoodsmarket.com

Index